Editorial Project Manager
Erica N. Russikoff, M.A.

Editor in Chief
Karen J. Goldfluss, M.S. Ed.

Creative Director
Sarah M. Fournier

Cover Artist
Sarah Kim

Imaging
Amanda R. Harter

Publisher
Mary D. Smith, M.S. Ed.

KNOW THE LINGO!
Mastering
Academic
Vocabulary

GRADE **2**

- Introduces a variety of strategies that help students learn the language of the classroom
- Provides practice with need-to-know academic vocabulary used in all subjects
- Improves students' ability to understand and follow directions
- Includes Lexile measures and standards correlations

Teacher Created Resources

Author
Tracie I. Heskett, M. Ed.

Teacher Created Resources
12621 Western Avenue
Garden Grove, CA 92841
www.teachercreated.com
ISBN: 978-1-4206-8132-1

© 2018 Teacher Created Resources
Made in U.S.A.

Teacher Created Resources

TABLE OF CONTENTS

INTRODUCTION

In order for students to acquire new knowledge and learning, they must be able to understand what they read, hear, and are asked to do in the classroom. According to Robert Marzano, a leading researcher in education and author of several books on academic vocabulary, students must comprehend academic vocabulary in order to understand instruction and academic texts. Often, students have a hard time writing to prompts or responding to instructions because they don't know exactly what is being asked. This is because they don't understand the meanings behind instructional verbs or how these words are used in an academic context.

What Is Academic Vocabulary?

Academic vocabulary is the language of the classroom. It includes academic language—the specific words and phrases that students encounter in their academic reading, assignments, and daily classroom activities—as well as the grammar and language structures that make up classroom discussions. Academic vocabulary incorporates words not always used in everyday conversation, and sentences may be more complex. In some cases, students encounter words that have different meanings than they do in other contexts.

Academic vocabulary refers to words and phrases that are used in the process of learning. Benjamin Bloom, an educational psychologist, worked with colleagues to create and publish a taxonomy that provides a framework for classroom instruction. Bloom's Taxonomy has been updated to reflect the action words students encounter in their learning while maintaining a hierarchy of higher-order thinking. Each level contains key words found in academic tasks for that level of critical thinking. Current standards emphasize the need for students to develop critical-thinking skills. Bloom's Taxonomy labels the levels of higher-order thinking as remembering, understanding, applying, analyzing, evaluating, and creating.

Teachers and students use academic language to discuss new knowledge and concepts, develop ideas, talk about texts, and engage in classroom activities. This book will focus on terms used specifically in classroom instruction. Many of these terms are included in Bloom's Taxonomy, which enables teachers to identify objectives and plan instruction that develop critical-thinking skills and to assess student learning. Direct instruction in academic vocabulary supports students by helping them understand what they are expected to do.

This book contains three main components: strategies to help teachers explain academic vocabulary; lessons that present definitions, examples, and practice of academic instructional verbs; and a glossary, which includes related, non-specific academic language to further develop students' working vocabulary.

HOW TO USE THIS BOOK

Know the Lingo! Mastering Academic Vocabulary contains strategies, specific lessons and activities, and a glossary to help teachers illustrate and teach instructional verbs and other academic vocabulary. Introduce and discuss the concept of academic vocabulary with students. Explain that in school, teachers ask students to do certain things in the classroom. When teachers tell students what to do or how to do something, we call these sentences *instructions* or *directions.* It is important for students to understand what the words used in directions mean, so they will be able to successfully do what is being asked. In these lessons, students will learn the meanings of words teachers use when giving instructions. Other times, students read words that tell them what to do; these are called *written directions.* When first starting these lessons, help students understand the nature of and expected response to a *prompt.* A prompt is a sentence that tells students which action to take. Review also the concept of *task,* meaning a specific piece of work to be done, often assigned by another person. The glossary lists additional academic vocabulary students encounter in the context of instruction, activities, and other classroom materials. Students need to understand the meanings of these words in order to successfully complete academic tasks within the classroom. Copy these pages for students and explain to them that they will keep their glossaries handy to help them understand academic words used in the prompts and tasks in the lessons.

The strategies and examples listed on "Strategies to Teach Academic Vocabulary" (pages 6–7) offer support for students who need additional assistance in making connections between words, their meanings, and expected actions. They may be used with various instructional verbs and other academic vocabulary to teach students and help them incorporate academic vocabulary into their daily learning.

The "Academic Instructional Verbs" section (pages 8–103) highlights grade-appropriate instructional verbs that students will find included in many prompts. These words include *describe, determine, evaluate,* and *summarize.* The word list is compiled from grade-level standards and Bloom's Taxonomy. Lessons are presented in an order that correlates to the frequency with which students might encounter the word. For example, most prompts ask students to "write," so that lesson is one of the first taught. Each verb is explained in the following ways:

- **Define:** Students are provided with a definition of the instructional verb.
- **Study:** Students are asked to review sample prompts and tasks that include the instructional verb as well as sample responses to the prompts and tasks.
- **Practice:** Students practice answering prompts and completing tasks that contain the instructional verb.
- **Check:** Students participate in a small-group or whole-class activity to confirm their understanding of the instructional verb.
- **Review:** Students are reminded of how the instructional verb is used.
- **Collaborate:** Students collaborate in pairs to further demonstrate their understanding of the instructional verb.

HOW TO USE THIS BOOK *(cont.)*

Preview each lesson to ensure you have the needed materials on hand. When this icon appears [✎], prepare or complete the activity as directed. Guide students through the sample prompts and sample answers provided in each lesson to help students understand the meaning of the academic verb. Then preview the practice prompts and tasks to which students will respond. Ensure students have the "Academic Concepts Glossary" (pages 104–108) for reference as they complete individual, whole-class, small-group, or paired activities. Designate a place for students to store their glossaries for easy access during classroom instruction and activities. Sometimes a sample prompt or activity includes a short reading passage for students. Most reading passages fall within the second-grade reading range based on Lexile measures (420L–650L) for this grade level. For further review, consider using this comprehension check format as a follow-up to the lesson activities:

CHECK YOUR WORK

Think about your answers to the following questions. Discuss your thoughts with a partner or other classmates, or write your responses in a journal entry.

- Did you know what to do?
- Was it easy or hard to understand what the word or phrase means?
- Could you tell someone else what to do if they heard this word?
- In your own words, what does this word mean?

Note: Any Common Core State Standards addressed in lesson activities are listed on pages 110–112.

ACADEMIC VOCABULARY NOTEBOOKS

Consider having students keep academic vocabulary notebooks. Notebooks will help students with word recognition in future encounters. Encourage students to refer to their notebooks during various cross-curricular activities.

- Create and maintain a class "journal" to observe and discuss academic vocabulary in practice throughout a school day.
- Have students copy the word and a simple definition for reference in small-group discussions and activities.
- Have students write observations and new information about academic vocabulary.
- Have students write comments about their experiences with academic vocabulary in classroom activities.
- Encourage students to make connections across content areas.
- Have students discuss and compare their observations with classmates.
- Have students compare terms within or between subject areas.
- Provide activities that engage students in using terms from their notebooks.
- Have students edit and revise their notebooks to reflect new learning.

STRATEGIES TO TEACH ACADEMIC VOCABULARY

Each lesson includes specific tasks and strategies to help students learn academic vocabulary. Refer to the following tips to provide additional support for students who have trouble grasping a vocabulary concept.

Strategy	Example
Consider the language expectations in the lesson and text before teaching.	What are students being asked to do in this lesson? What academic vocabulary is embedded in the text?
Check which words students need to know in order to understand any instructions in the lesson.	Underline or highlight academic instructional verbs in the lesson instructions. Check for student understanding before teaching the lesson.
Evaluate what students already know about the terms.	Do they know what the word means? Do they know how to perform the action?
Review words and phrases with students to add to their knowledge base.	Point out different types of responses students make during classroom activities to broaden their understanding of the term.
Make sure students understand the words in directions or assignments.	Read a direction aloud. Ask students to verbally *describe* what they would do to complete that direction, in their own words, if possible.
Model how to use sentence starters to practice completing a writing prompt.	Think aloud to *discuss* the purposes of informational text. The main idea of this piece is _____. In this text, I learned that _____.
Provide pictorial representation with the definition of a word when possible.	Show pictures in a logical order (e.g., morning, noon, and night) to *define* sequential order.
Provide students with a description, example, or explanation when giving a formal definition of a word or phrase.	Show students a simple diagram to define a word such as *distinguish*: Draw two circles and explain that we can list characteristics of two things or ideas to tell how they are different.
Have students draw a picture or create a symbol or other graphic to represent the term.	Students might draw arrows to help them remember what to do when they *predict* or *review*.
Have students state their own descriptions, examples, or explanations.	Ask students to *demonstrate* and *give examples of* what it means to *identify* an author's purpose, a topic, or the way words are used to convey specific meaning.

STRATEGIES TO TEACH ACADEMIC VOCABULARY *(cont.)*

Strategy	Example
Break objectives and prompts down into parts to guide students.	Break a prompt such as "Use evidence from informational texts to support your analysis, reflection, and research of a topic" into separate questions: What did you find (evidence) in your research to support the new information you have learned about your topic? How did these facts, details, definitions, examples, and reasons (evidence) help you better understand your topic?
Consider having EL students write definitions in their native language.	*describer: explicar con detalle las características de algo o alguien* (to describe: explain with detail the characteristics of something or someone) Compare to our definition: to *describe* means to create a picture of something in words
Incorporate student practice with vocabulary words and language structures during collaborative or independent work.	Have students explore working definitions of a verb such as *discuss* and act out/practice what they have learned.
Have students discuss new terms with each other.	Encourage students to discuss what it means to *evaluate* and *give examples of* when they have done this.
Include games along with vocabulary activities.	Students may enjoy playing games, such as a matching memory game or a beanbag toss, to learn the meanings of words.
Help students make connections between academic words and what they are expected to do or know how to do.	Consider having students generate a chart listing several instructional verbs with a picture next to each verb illustrating what a student would do to perform that action.
Refer to specific academic vocabulary and its meanings in everyday activities.	If students are making a class decision, ask individuals what they might say to *convince* classmates to consider their ideas.
Teach language and content together when applicable.	Provide examples of what it means to *report* in a variety of contexts (e.g., science or social studies).
Brainstorm with students ways they could complete a specific prompt or task.	Conduct a class discussion to create a web or chart listing ways students could develop a topic, or how they could include text features and illustrations to increase reader comprehension.

Name: _____

TELL

 DEFINE

Question: What does it mean to <u>tell</u> something?
Answer: When we <u>tell</u> something, we put it into words. We might say what happened or give a story.

 STUDY

Sample Prompt: Use words to <u>tell</u> about a holiday we celebrate in the fall.
Sample Answer: We have Thanksgiving in the fall.

Sample Prompt: <u>Tell</u> one thing you like about holidays.
Sample Answer: On a holiday, people might not have to go to school or work.

✎ **PRACTICE**

① **Prompt:** <u>Tell</u> about your favorite holiday. Why do you like it?

_____

_____

_____

② **Prompt:** Use words to <u>tell</u> some things people do on holidays in the winter.

_____

_____

_____

③ **Prompt:** What details might you <u>tell</u> in a story about a holiday?

_____

_____

_____

④ **Prompt:** <u>Tell</u> about something you and your classmates did to celebrate a special day.
After you put the words on the lines below, say them to one or more classmates.

_____

_____

TELL (cont.)

☑ CHECK

Look back at what the word <u>tell</u> means.

① Discuss together with classmates things you like about holidays.

② Work with your teacher to create a web. 🖊

③ Take turns with classmates saying words to put in the web to <u>tell</u> things you like about holidays.

🔍 REVIEW

- When we <u>tell</u> about something, we give information about it.
- We <u>tell</u> what happened when we give a report.
- We can <u>tell</u> a story by putting it into words.

💬 COLLABORATE

When we look back at what this word means, we see that it means to say or write words about something.

① <u>Tell</u> a classmate about your favorite holiday and why you like it. Read the words you used in Practice Prompt #1.

② Listen to your classmate <u>tell</u> about his or her favorite holiday.

③ Work with your classmate to <u>tell</u> a story about a favorite holiday. Help each other put words on paper so other people can read your story.

_____

_____

_____

_____

_____

_____

_____

_____

Name: _____

WRITE

 DEFINE

Question: What does it mean to <u>write</u>?
Answer: When we <u>write</u>, we use a pencil or pen to put words on paper. We can <u>write</u> stories, articles, poems, and other things.

 STUDY

Sample Prompt: <u>Write</u> a sentence about a place you like to visit.
Sample Answer: I like to go to the park.

Sample Prompt: <u>Write</u> about a place you would like to see.
Sample Answer: I would like to see the ocean.

✏️ **PRACTICE**

① **Prompt:** <u>Write</u> a sentence about a place you would like to visit.

_____

_____

② **Task:** Which word did you <u>write</u> that tells the place you want to see? Circle the word you put down on paper in Practice Prompt #1 that names that place.

③ **Prompt:** <u>Write</u> two or three sentences about an interesting place you have been.

_____

_____

_____

☑ **CHECK**

Look back at what the word <u>write</u> means.

① On a piece of paper or individual whiteboard, <u>write</u> words to tell about an interesting place to visit.

② Share your words with a small group of classmates.

③ Work together as a group to <u>write</u> several sentences about why this place is interesting to visit. Use a separate piece of paper.

WRITE *(cont.)*

REVIEW

- We <u>write</u> when we use a pencil or pen to put words on paper.
- We can <u>write</u> stories, articles, poems, and other things.
- When we <u>write</u>, we communicate using words on paper.

COLLABORATE

When we look back at what this word means, we see that it means to put words on paper.

① <u>Write</u> clues about the interesting place you wrote about in Practice Prompt #3.
(*Note:* A clue gives a hint without telling the answer.)

_____

_____

_____

_____

_____

_____

_____

② Read your clues to a classmate. Ask your classmate to <u>write</u> down what place he or she thinks you visited. Use a separate piece of paper.

③ <u>Write</u> why you would or would not like to visit the place your classmate wrote about.

_____

_____

_____

_____

_____

_____

Name: _____

DEFINE

DEFINE

Question: What does it mean to <u>define</u> something?

Answer: When we <u>define</u> something, we tell what it means. We describe or explain it exactly.

STUDY

Sample Prompt: <u>Define</u> the word *river*.

Sample Answer: A river is a large body of water that flows into a lake or ocean.

Sample Prompt: Write a sentence to <u>define</u> a *valley*.

Sample Answer: A valley is an area of low ground between two hills.

PRACTICE

① **Prompt:** How would you <u>define</u> a mountain?

_____

_____

② **Task:** Read the sentences below. Underline the words that <u>define</u> the landform.

   A plateau is a large area of high, flat land. It is higher than the other land around it.

③ **Prompt:** <u>Define</u> the word *landform*. Write one or two sentences to tell what this word means.

_____

_____

☑ CHECK

Look back at what the word <u>define</u> means.

① Read the sentences below. Put a check mark by each sentence that tells how to <u>define</u> a word.

   ☐ Read the words around the word to figure out what it means.

   ☐ Look at a picture.

   ☐ Act out the word.

   ☐ Write the word in a sentence.

   ☐ Look up the word in a dictionary.

   ☐ Ask a friend what the word means.

② Share your answers with the class.

DEFINE (cont.)

🔍 REVIEW

- When we <u>define</u> a word, we state the meaning.
- We can <u>define</u> words to show that we know exactly what they mean.
- We can <u>define</u> something by describing it exactly.

💬 COLLABORATE

When we look back at what this word means, we see that it means to say the meaning of a word.

① Work with a classmate to draw a line from each landform on the left to the words on the right that <u>define</u> it.

coast	a raised area of land that is smaller than a mountain
hill	an area of low ground between two hills, often with a river flowing through it
island	a large, flat area of land
plain	a piece of land with water all around it
valley	the land that is next to the sea

② Use a dictionary to check words you do not know from the box above.

③ Tell your classmate one thing you have learned about how to <u>define</u> words.

④ What did you learn from your classmate about how to <u>define</u>?

_____

_____

_____

_____

_____

Name: _____

PRACTICE

DEFINE

Question: What does it mean to <u>practice</u> something?
Answer: When we <u>practice</u> something, we repeat an action so we will get better at that skill. We <u>practice</u> something when we put it into action.

STUDY

Sample Prompt: <u>Practice</u> writing a complete sentence about a color.
Sample Answer: Red is a primary color.

Sample Prompt: <u>Practice</u> answering this prompt: What colors make you happy?
Sample Answer: Yellow makes me happy because it reminds me of the sun, and 1 like sunshine.

✎ PRACTICE

① **Prompt:** <u>Practice</u> answering this prompt: What is your favorite color, and why do you like it?

_____

_____

_____

_____

② **Prompt:** <u>Practice</u> writing two or three sentences about the colors you see in the classroom.

_____

_____

_____

_____

_____

③ **Task:** <u>Practice</u> making a pattern by coloring the circles different colors.

◯ ◯ ◯ ◯ ◯ ◯ ◯

PRACTICE *(cont.)*

☑ CHECK

Look back at what the word <u>practice</u> means.

① How can we <u>practice</u> following directions? Write one or two sentences on the lines.

_____

_____

② Share your ideas with two other classmates in a group of three.

③ Share one idea from your small group with the class.

🔍 REVIEW

- We do an action several times to <u>practice</u> and get better at something.
- We can put a plan into <u>practice</u> by putting it into action.
- We <u>practice</u> answering prompts to learn how to write better.

💬 COLLABORATE

When we look back at what this word means, we see that it means to do something more than once to learn how to do it better.

① <u>Practice</u> creating a pattern with different shapes. Leave blank spaces in your pattern for a classmate to complete. Then switch pages with a classmate to complete each other's patterns.

② Write a prompt about colors for your partner to <u>practice</u> answering.

_____

_____

③ <u>Practice</u> answering the prompt your partner wrote.

_____

_____

Name: _____

REVIEW

 DEFINE

Question: What does it mean to <u>review</u>?
Answer: When we <u>review</u>, we study or go over something again. We look at something carefully to see if any changes are necessary.

 STUDY

Sample Task: <u>Review</u> what you know about coins and write a sentence.
Sample Answer: We use coins to buy things we need or want.

Sample Task: <u>Review</u> the sentence and underline what you would change to make the sentence correct.
Sample Answer: <u>a</u> nickel is worth <u>fiv</u> cents.

✎ **PRACTICE**

① **Prompt:** <u>Review</u> what you already know about money and write your ideas on the lines.

_____

_____

_____

② **Task:** Read the paragraph.

People use money to buy things that someone else is selling. Things cost different amounts of money. We use coins and paper bills for money. Most paper bills are worth more than coins. Some people save their coins. They wait until they have enough coins to buy something they want.

③ **Task:** <u>Review</u> what the text above says about money. What is one thing you learned?

_____

_____

_____

④ **Task:** <u>Review</u> the sentence below. Make changes so it is correct. Write the corrected sentence on the line.

A pencil costs about tin cents

_____

REVIEW *(cont.)*

☑ CHECK

Look back at what the word <u>review</u> means.

① Listen as your teacher asks you and your classmates questions about what it means to <u>review</u>. 🖉

② Answer one of these questions when it's your turn:
  - What does it mean to <u>review</u> a text?
  - What do we do when we <u>review</u> a sentence?
  - What did we <u>review</u> in class this morning?
  - Why do we <u>review</u> what we learn?

🔍 REVIEW

- We <u>review</u> something by studying or going over it again.
- We can <u>review</u> something to see if it needs any changes.

💬 COLLABORATE

When we look back at what this word means, we see that it means to look at something again. Sometimes we check to see if it needs any changes.

① Which of your responses to the practice prompt and practice tasks will you <u>review</u>?

_____

_____

_____

② What will you do to <u>review</u> your response?

_____

_____

_____

③ Talk about your answers with a partner. What have you learned about what it means to <u>review</u>?

_____

_____

_____

Name: _____

TAKE NOTES

 DEFINE

Question: What does it mean to <u>take notes</u>?
Answer: When we <u>take notes</u>, we get information from something we hear or read. We write what we learn.

 STUDY

Sample Prompt: <u>Take notes</u> about what you have already heard or read about ocean life.
Sample Answer: Many different kinds of animals live in the ocean. Some have very bright colors.

Sample Prompt: Read the sentences below and <u>take notes</u> about the facts you notice.

Some ocean animals live in very deep water. Sunlight does not reach these animals.
Sample Answer: Some ocean animals live in darkness because the water is too deep for sunlight.

✎ **PRACTICE**

① **Prompt:** Think about what you already know and have heard about ocean life. <u>Take notes</u> about what you remember.

_____

_____

_____

_____

② **Prompt:** Read the sentences below. <u>Take notes</u> on what you learn from what you read.

Did you know there are slugs in the ocean? These tiny animals are less than an inch long. They are very colorful. Some have gills to breathe. Others have organs on their backs to breathe. They do not have shells to protect themselves from enemies. Their bright colors give other animals a warning. These slugs can take poison from other animals and use it on their enemies!

_____

_____

_____

_____

TAKE NOTES *(cont.)*

☑ CHECK

Look back at what it means to <u>take notes</u>.

① Listen as your teacher reads a short paragraph about ocean life. 🖊

② <u>Take notes</u> about what you hear and learn. Use a separate piece of paper.

③ Take turns sharing your notes with a small group.

④ With your group, discuss what you learned about <u>taking notes</u> from hearing your classmates' notes.

⑤ Why is it important to learn to <u>take notes</u>? How does this help us learn new information? Talk about your ideas with your small group.

🔍 REVIEW

- We <u>take notes</u> when we write information from something we hear or read.
- When we <u>take notes</u>, we write the main ideas from what we read.
- We can include drawings and words when we <u>take notes</u> to help us remember what we learn.

💬 COLLABORATE

When we look back at what it means to <u>take notes</u>, we see that it means to write information we learn from something we hear or read.

① Answer the questions below.

Think of a time when you <u>took notes</u>. What did you want to learn or remember? Why?

_____

_____

How do we use this term, <u>take notes</u>, in our classroom?

_____

_____

How can <u>taking notes</u> help us when we need to answer a question or solve a problem?

_____

_____

② Discuss your notes for #1 with a partner.

Name: _____

REPORT

 DEFINE

Question: What does it mean to <u>report</u>?
Answer: When we <u>report</u>, we write or tell what happened.

 STUDY

Sample Prompt: <u>Report</u> on a school meeting.
Sample Answer: Yesterday, we had a meeting at school. All the students came. The meeting was about bullying.

Sample Prompt: <u>Report</u> on an event that happened at your school.
Sample Answer: Last week, parents and friends came for Dr. Seuss Reading Day at our school.

PRACTICE

① **Prompt:** <u>Report</u> on something that happened in your classroom today.

_____

_____

_____

_____

② **Prompt:** <u>Report</u> on a recent visit to the school library.

_____

_____

_____

_____

③ **Task:** Learn about another school. <u>Report</u> what you learned.

_____

_____

_____

_____

REPORT (cont.)

☑ CHECK

Look back at what the word report means.

① Work in a small group to talk about the information a person should include when he or she reports about a person, place, or event.

② As a group, write your ideas on a separate piece of paper.

③ Report your ideas to the class. Work together with your teacher to create a list of guidelines for you and your classmates to follow when you report on a person, place, or event. 📝

🔍 REVIEW

- We report when we say or write what happened.
- When we report, we give a detailed statement about something that happened.
- When we report about something, we give information about it.
- We tell people about something when we report.
- When we report, we might describe our feelings about a thing or event.

💬 COLLABORATE

When we look back at what this word means, we see that it means to say or write details or information about something.

① Review the information you reported about another school in Practice Task #3.

② Report what you learned to a classmate.

③ Listen as your partner reports to you what he or she learned. Give your partner feedback by asking questions about the information he or she reported.

EXPLAIN

📖 DEFINE

Question: What does it mean to explain something?

Answer: When we explain something, we make it clear so that it is easier to understand.

👤 STUDY

Sample Prompt: How would you explain a computer game?

Sample Answer: A computer game is played on a computer. Players take part in the game by pressing keys on a keyboard. Players see the action in the game on a screen.

Sample Prompt: Explain how to play a role-playing game.

Sample Answer: In a role-playing game, players pretend to be characters in the game. They act out what the characters do in the game.

✏️ PRACTICE

① **Prompt:** Explain your favorite game. (Think about what the game is like and how to play it.)

_____

_____

② **Task:** Draw a picture to explain your answer to Practice Prompt #1.

③ **Prompt:** Explain how you play a card game. (You can choose any game.)

_____

_____

④ **Prompt:** Explain why you do or do not like computer games.

_____

_____

EXPLAIN *(cont.)*

☑ CHECK

Look back at what the word <u>explain</u> means.

① How would you <u>explain</u> the first sample answer in the Study section on page 22? What would you add to it to make it easier to understand? Write your ideas on the lines below.

_____

_____

_____

_____

_____

_____

② Turn and share your ideas with a classmate.

③ Talk with a different classmate. <u>Explain</u> what you learned from the first classmate.

🔍 REVIEW

- We <u>explain</u> something when we make it clear and easy to understand.
- We can <u>explain</u> something by telling what it means.
- We <u>explain</u> something when we give information.
- When we <u>explain</u> something, we tell or show the reason for it.

💬 COLLABORATE

When we look back at what this word means, we see that it means to give information to make something easy to understand.

① Think about how you would <u>explain</u> how pictures add to a board game.

② Show a classmate your drawing from Practice Task #2. Ask your partner to <u>explain</u> how the picture helps him or her understand your answer for Practice Prompt #1.

③ What would you like your partner to <u>explain</u> more to help you understand his or her favorite game and why it is a favorite? Share your answer with your partner.

Name: _____

DEVELOP

DEFINE

Question: What does it mean to <u>develop</u> something?
Answer: When we <u>develop</u> something, we build on an idea. We might add facts and other information to <u>develop</u> a topic.

STUDY

Sample Prompt: Use facts and information to <u>develop</u> the topic of what you know about weather.
Sample Answer: When drops of water fall from the sky, we say it is raining. The rain can be heavy, like water spilled from a bucket. It can be very light, like a mist. Rain makes puddles on the ground.

Sample Prompt: Add details to <u>develop</u> your ideas about why people like to play in the snow.
Sample Answer: Kids like to play in the snow. Snow makes everything look and sound different. It is fun to slide down a hill in the snow. Sometimes people throw snowballs. In the snow, you can build a snowman or snow fort.

PRACTICE

① **Prompt:** How does weather affect what we do each day?

_____

_____

_____

② **Task:** <u>Develop</u> your ideas about how weather affects what we do each day. Think about facts and information you could add to your answer for Practice Prompt #1. Write one or two sentences to <u>develop</u> the topic of how weather affects us.

_____

_____

_____

③ **Prompt:** What details can you add to your writing to further <u>develop</u> your ideas about the topic?

_____

_____

_____

DEVELOP (cont.)

☑ CHECK

Look back at what the word <u>develop</u> means.

① Sometimes clouds build when a storm <u>develops</u>. What is one thing you can say about watching storms? Write your idea in box #1 of the chart below.

② Share your idea with a classmate. Write your partner's idea in box #2 of the chart.

③ Think about what your classmate shared. Write a new idea in box #3 of the chart to <u>develop</u> your thoughts about storms.

④ Share your idea with a different classmate. Listen to your classmate's idea and write it in box #4 of the chart.

My Ideas	A Classmate's Ideas
1	2
3	4

🔍 REVIEW

- We <u>develop</u> a subject by adding more information about it.
- We can <u>develop</u> our ideas about a topic by adding more details to make our writing clear and easy to read.
- When we <u>develop</u> our ideas, we make them stronger and more effective.
- We can use facts and information to <u>develop</u> what we want to say.

💬 COLLABORATE

When we look back at what this word means, we see that it means to add more information about a subject.

① Discuss with a different classmate how you can <u>develop</u> the topic of predicting the weather.

② <u>Develop</u> your ideas about this topic. Write one or two sentences about what you already know about tools people use and other ways people predict the weather. Use a separate piece of paper.

③ Share your sentences with your partner. Give him or her one suggestion about how to <u>develop</u> his or her writing to make it stronger.

SUPPORT

DEFINE

Question: What does it mean to <u>support</u> something?

Answer: When we <u>support</u> something, we show it to be true. We give reasons to <u>support</u> what we think or believe about something to convince others to agree with us.

STUDY

Sample Prompt: What facts or information can you give to <u>support</u> the statement that yogurt is a good food to eat?

Sample Answer: Yogurt is a healthy food that comes in different flavors.

Sample Prompt: What is a reason that <u>supports</u> eating blueberries?

Sample Answer: Some people like to eat blueberries because they are sweet. Also, they are easy to eat. You do not have to peel or cut them.

✏️ PRACTICE

① **Task:** Read the opinion statement below. Circle the letter next to the sentence that gives a reason to <u>support</u> the opinion.

Opinion statement: On a cold day, my favorite food to eat is tomato soup.

   a. I have to eat it quickly so it doesn't melt.

   b. Tomato soup is easy to eat.

   c. Tomato soup is hot, and it tastes good on a cold day.

   d. My favorite crackers are whole wheat.

② **Prompt:** What is your favorite food, and why do you like it? Give reasons to <u>support</u> your opinion.

_____

_____

_____

③ **Prompt:** How do your reasons <u>support</u> what you say about your favorite food?

_____

_____

_____

SUPPORT (cont.)

☑ CHECK

Look back at what the word <u>support</u> means.

① Talk with classmates in a small group about a food that you like. Then work together to write a statement about that food.

② On a slip of paper, write a reason to say why you might like that food.

③ Put your reason together with the reasons from others in your group.

④ Trade your statement about food and your group's reasons with another group.

⑤ How well do the reasons from the other group <u>support</u> their statement about a food they like? Share your answer with your group.

⑥ What facts and information does the other group give to <u>support</u> what they say so that it makes sense? Share your answer with your group.

🔍 REVIEW

- We can <u>support</u> our ideas by giving facts and information to show what we say makes sense.
- We can give reasons to <u>support</u> our opinion about something.
- When we <u>support</u> something, we show it to be true.

💬 COLLABORATE

When we look back at what this word means, we see that it means to give reasons to show why something might be true.

Read the paragraph below.

> Apples are one of my favorite foods. I like things that are crunchy. Raw apple slices are crunchy. On a cold day, heated applesauce warms me up. It tastes good with cinnamon. Cooked apples with toasted oats make a quick, tasty breakfast. There are so many good ways to eat apples!

① What is the main idea of this paragraph?

_____

_____

② Underline the reasons in the paragraph that <u>support</u> the main idea.

③ Discuss with a partner which reasons <u>support</u> the main idea.

Name: _____

PRODUCE

 ## DEFINE

Question: What does it mean to <u>produce</u> something?
Answer: When we <u>produce</u> something, we make something.

 ## STUDY

Sample Prompt: What does a music band <u>produce</u>?
Sample Answer: A music band produces different sounds that make music.

Sample Prompt: <u>Produce</u> a sentence about a parade band.
Sample Answer: A parade band has people that march and play drums.

 ## PRACTICE

① **Prompt:** <u>Produce</u> a complete sentence about a sound we hear.

_____

_____

② **Task:** Think about a story idea that has that sound and other sounds in it. <u>Produce</u> one or more sounds that might be part of the story. How would you write those sounds on paper?

_____

③ **Prompt:** Write your sentences and ideas from Practice Prompt #1 and Practice Task #2 to <u>produce</u> a story.

_____

_____

_____

_____

_____

_____

_____

_____

PRODUCE *(cont.)*

☑ CHECK

Look back at what the word <u>produce</u> means.

① If possible, use a document camera or interactive whiteboard to share with classmates the story you <u>produced</u> for Practice Prompt #3. 📝

② Ask classmates to <u>produce</u> feedback to help you strengthen your writing.

③ Use tools such as a pen or highlighter to <u>produce</u> feedback for classmates.

🔍 REVIEW

- We <u>produce</u> something when we make or create something.
- When we <u>produce</u> something, we make it happen.
- When we <u>produce</u> something, we might show it to someone else.
- Sometimes when we <u>produce</u> something, we provide something that is needed.

💬 COLLABORATE

When we look back at what this word means, we see that it means to create or make something.

① Work with a classmate to learn more about a type of music you both enjoy.

② <u>Produce</u> sentences to report on what you learned.

_____

_____

_____

③ Talk with your partner about the best way to share your sentences with others in the class. Write your ideas on the lines below.

_____

_____

_____

_____

④ Use digital tools to <u>produce</u> and publish your writing.

Name: _____

DESCRIBE

 DEFINE

Question: What does it mean to <u>describe</u> something?
Answer: When we <u>describe</u> something, we create a picture of something with words.

 STUDY

Sample Text: Pete's backyard is overgrown with weeds. No one takes care of it. There is trash everywhere. The trash attracts many insects and rodents.
Sample Prompt: <u>Describe</u> the backyard in the sample text.
Sample Answer: Pete's backyard is not nice to look at. You can't see any flowers or bushes because there are so many weeds. There is also a lot of trash and bugs.

Sample Prompt: <u>Describe</u> what the sky looks like.
Sample Answer: When the sun is out, the sky is blue. There are usually many white clouds in the sky. Sometimes you can see birds fly.

 PRACTICE

① **Task:** Read the story below. Then answer the prompts.

James pulled the covers over his head as the wind howled outside. By the next morning, the wind had stopped. James went outside to look around. He saw leaves and tree branches on the ground. The wind had blown bits of paper and other trash everywhere. Then James went to look at the backyard. The wind had torn a board off of Oscar's doghouse. Now there was a huge hole in the side of the doghouse. James found the board and set it next to the doghouse to cover the hole. He would ask his dad to fix it so Oscar would be warm again.

② **Prompt:** <u>Describe</u> where the story takes place.

_____

_____

③ **Prompt:** <u>Describe</u> the main character in the story.

_____

_____

④ **Prompt:** <u>Describe</u> Oscar's doghouse.

_____

_____

DESCRIBE *(cont.)*

☑ CHECK

Look back at what the word <u>describe</u> means.

① Your teacher will display a blank web. 📝

② Work together with classmates to <u>describe</u> the place where you have recess.

③ Take turns writing your responses on the web.

④ Also <u>describe</u> the people and things you see in this place. With classmates, add your ideas to the web.

🔍 REVIEW

· To <u>describe</u> something means to create a picture with words.

· We can <u>describe</u> where a story takes place. We can also <u>describe</u> people and things in a story.

· We give details when we <u>describe</u> something.

· We can <u>describe</u> a person, place, or thing.

💬 COLLABORATE

When we look back at what this word means, we see that it means to create a picture of something with words.

① Trade your answer to Practice Prompt #2 with a partner.

② Read your partner's answer to Practice Prompt #2.

③ Draw a picture of what your partner <u>described</u> in his or her answer. Use a separate piece of paper.

④ Look at the picture your partner drew for your answer.

⑤ How well did you <u>describe</u> where the story takes place?

_____

_____

_____

_____

_____

Name: _____

PLAN

 DEFINE

Question: What does it mean to <u>plan</u> something?
Answer: When we <u>plan</u> something, we work out ahead of time how we will do it. When we <u>plan</u> to do something, we expect to do it.

 STUDY

Sample Prompt: <u>Plan</u> what you will do to take care of your pet tomorrow.
Sample Answer: Tomorrow, I will make sure my hamster has food and water.

Sample Prompt: <u>Plan</u> the best time to take a dog to the dog park.
Sample Answer: I think the best time to go to the dog park is after school when it is still light out.

✏️ **PRACTICE**

① **Prompt:** What would it be like to have a pet in a second-grade classroom? Think about the best kind of pet and <u>plan</u> how students would work together to take care of it.

_____

_____

_____

② **Prompt:** <u>Plan</u> how you might choose the best pet for your family. What details and questions would you think about?

_____

_____

_____

_____

③ **Prompt:** <u>Plan</u> what to do with your pet when you go on vacation.

_____

_____

_____

_____

PLAN *(cont.)*

☑ CHECK

Look back at what the word <u>plan</u> means.

① Work with a small group to <u>plan</u> a pet fair. Write questions you will answer as you <u>plan</u>. (Think about *what, when, where, why, who,* and *how* questions.) Use a separate piece of paper.

② Talk with others in your group to answer the questions you wrote on the separate piece of paper. This will help you <u>plan</u> your imaginary pet fair. As you <u>plan</u>, take notes on the same piece of paper.

③ Share your ideas with the class. Ask other classmates to help you <u>plan</u> ways to make the pet fair a great success.

REVIEW

- When we <u>plan</u> to do something, we mean to do it.
- When we <u>plan</u> something, we think about and arrange the parts or details before it happens or before it is made.

COLLABORATE

When we look back at what this word means, we see that it means to think about and say or write how we will do something.

① <u>Plan</u> how you would train a puppy. What would you like the dog to do? Write the steps you would take to teach the puppy.

_____

_____

_____

_____

_____

_____

② Draw a picture to show what you <u>plan</u> to do to train a puppy. Use a separate piece of paper.

③ Ask your partner how you could <u>plan</u> better to make sure the puppy is well trained.

Name: _____

IDENTIFY

 DEFINE

Question: What does it mean to <u>identify</u> something?

Answer: When we <u>identify</u> something, we recognize or tell what something is.

 STUDY

Sample Prompt: <u>Identify</u> the meaning of the underlined word in the sentence below.

In Brazil, people like to have green <u>peas</u> on their pizza.

Sample Answer: a. a fruit   b. a drink   c. a vegetable   d. a meat

Sample Prompt: <u>Identify</u> how we usually use these words: *spicy, juicy, tasty*.

Sample Answer: We often use these words to describe foods.

✎ **PRACTICE**

① **Task:** Read the paragraph below. Then <u>identify</u> the main topic of the paragraph. Write the main topic on the lines.

People like to make their food interesting. They try different foods together to see how it tastes. Some foods we like together may seem strange to other people. When we put different foods together, it may create a new dish. A good example of this is putting strawberries on a spinach salad. People often think about putting only vegetables on salads. To put fruit on a vegetable salad is different. It makes a new dish.

_____

_____

_____

② **Prompt:** Write a story about an unusual food that a character has tried or would like to try. Include a problem in your story. Use a separate piece of paper.

③ **Task:** <u>Identify</u> the first verb in Practice Prompt #2 that tells what you will do. Underline that word.

IDENTIFY *(cont.)*

☑ CHECK

Look back at what the word <u>identify</u> means.

① Review the paragraph in Practice Task #1.

② Which words or phrases helped you <u>identify</u> the topic of the paragraph?

_____

③ Talk with classmates to <u>identify</u> why the author wrote this paragraph. What did the author want to answer, explain, or describe?

④ Which words or phrases help you <u>identify</u> the reason the author wrote this piece?

_____

◯ REVIEW

- When we <u>identify</u> something, we know and say what it is.
- We <u>identify</u> something when we find out what it is.
- We can <u>identify</u> something by showing what it is.

💬 COLLABORATE

When we look back at what this word means, we see that it means to show or say what something is.

① Read the story a classmate wrote for Practice Prompt #2.

② Highlight words and phrases that help you <u>identify</u> the main topic of the story.

③ <u>Identify</u> the problem a character has in the story.

_____

_____

_____

④ <u>Identify</u> how the character in the story solves his or her problem.

_____

_____

Name: _____

DETERMINE

 ## DEFINE

Question: What does it mean to <u>determine</u> something?
Answer: When we <u>determine</u> something, we find out or discover it.

 ## STUDY

Sample Prompt: <u>Determine</u> the meaning of the word *punctuation.*
Sample Answer: Punctuation means periods, commas, and other marks we use to make writing clear.

Sample Prompt: <u>Determine</u> which word means the opposite of *dry.*
Sample Answer:

> cold   sunny   (rainy)   smooth   warm

✏ PRACTICE

① **Prompt:** How can we <u>determine</u> the meaning of a word?

_____

_____

② **Task:** <u>Determine</u> which word has a similar meaning to *leafy.* Circle the word which means almost the same as *leafy.*

> bushy   shady   cool   sandy   smoky

How did you <u>determine</u> which word has a similar meaning?

_____

_____

③ **Task:** <u>Determine</u> if each sentence is correct. Think about what you know about conventions. Look at capitalization, punctuation, and spelling. Draw a check mark by each sentence that has a mistake in it. Then fix the mistake to make the sentence correct.

_____ 1. Animals adapt to were they live.

_____ 2. a habitat is a place where an animal lives.

_____ 3. Living things need air water, food, and shelter.

_____ 4. Plants are an important part of an animal's habitat.

_____ 5. Some people work to save places where animals live

DETERMINE (cont.)

☑ CHECK

Look back at what the word <u>determine</u> means.

Your teacher will ask the class questions. Take turns answering the following questions as your teacher tosses a beanbag to you and your classmates. 🖊

- How can we <u>determine</u> the meaning of a word we do not know?
- How can we <u>determine</u> the topic of a text?
- How can we <u>determine</u> the author's main idea in a story?
- How can we <u>determine</u> the answer to a problem?

🔍 REVIEW

- We can study a text to <u>determine</u> certain things about it.
- When we solve a problem, we <u>determine</u> or find the answer to it.
- We can <u>determine</u> the meanings of words by reading and talking with others to help our understanding.

💬 COLLABORATE

When we look back at what this word means, we see that it means to find out about something.

① Think about how we <u>determine</u> the meanings of words we do not know.

② Work with a partner to <u>determine</u> the meanings of the words in the chart. Use the tip given for each word to help you.

③ Write the meaning of each word on a separate piece of paper.

Word	Tip
Caves are <u>moist</u> and damp because the sun does not dry any rain that drips into the cave.	Look at other words in the sentence as clues to <u>determine</u> the meaning of a new word.
untrained	Think about the new meaning of the word when a prefix is added to it.
poisonous	Look to see if there is a word you know within the new word.
waterfall	Use what you know about each word to <u>determine</u> the meaning of a compound word.
environment	Use a dictionary.
shelter	Use a glossary.

Name: _____

ANSWER

DEFINE

Question: What does it mean to give an <u>answer</u> or to <u>answer</u> a question?

Answer: When we give an <u>answer</u>, we say or write something in reply to a question, to something someone says, or to something we read.

STUDY

Sample Prompt: Read the question and <u>answer</u> the prompt. <u>Answer</u> with a complete sentence.

What do we use to type on a computer?

Sample Answer: We use a keyboard to type on a computer.

Sample Prompt: How would you <u>answer</u> this question: What tasks might someone do on a computer?

Sample Answer: People write stories on a computer. They send emails. They can also read things on the Internet.

✏️ PRACTICE

① **Prompt:** Read the question and <u>answer</u> the prompt. <u>Answer</u> with a complete sentence. How do students in your class use computers?

_____

_____

_____

② **Prompt:** Read the question and <u>answer</u> the prompt. <u>Answer</u> with a complete sentence. What technology do you see in your classroom?

_____

_____

_____

③ **Prompt:** How would you <u>answer</u> this question: What is your favorite thing to do on a computer?

_____

_____

_____

ANSWER (cont.)

☑ CHECK

Look back at what the word <u>answer</u> means.

① What problems can computers solve for people? Write your <u>answer</u> on the lines.

_____

_____

_____

_____

② Read aloud how you <u>answered</u> the question as part of a class discussion.

③ After you hear how your classmates <u>answered</u> the question, share any new ideas you have.

🔍 REVIEW

- An <u>answer</u> is something that is said or written in reply to a question.
- When we choose the best <u>answer</u>, we look for the best or most correct reply to the question.
- We might be asked to <u>answer</u> a question with a complete sentence.
- An <u>answer</u> can be a solution to a problem.

💬 COLLABORATE

When we look back at what this word means, we see that it can mean to say or write something in reply to a question.

① Write your <u>answers</u> to these questions on a separate piece of paper:
  - What jobs can robots do?
  - Why are people interested in robots?

② Ask a partner how he or she <u>answered</u> the questions.

③ What did you learn about how to <u>answer</u> questions from talking with your partner?

_____

_____

_____

_____

Name: _____

STATE

 DEFINE

Question: What does it mean to <u>state</u> something?

Answer: When we <u>state</u> something, we say or write it in words. We tell or explain something.

 STUDY

Sample Prompt: <u>State</u> the author's opinion in the sentence below.

Not all dinosaurs have died out; some animals that are like dinosaurs are still alive today.

Sample Answer: Some animals today are like dinosaurs.

Sample Prompt: <u>State</u> the main idea of the text below.

Most dinosaurs we read about lived on land. But at least one lived in the water. The *spinosaurus* swam in the rivers of ancient Africa. It had nostrils on top of its snout. It could swim and still breathe air. This dinosaur's bones helped it float. It ate fish in the river.

Sample Answer: The spinosaurus was a dinosaur that lived in the water.

 PRACTICE

① **Prompt:** <u>State</u> the main idea of the paragraph below.

Woolly mammoths lived a very long time ago. Scientists think they are closely related to elephants. These large land animals lived in cold places. They had thick, shaggy coats. Their ears were smaller than elephants' ears and were close to their heads. These things helped them live in the harsh winters. When the weather got warmer, they could not survive.

_____

_____

_____

② **Prompt:** Why are dinosaurs no longer alive? <u>State</u> your opinion (what you think).

_____

_____

_____

_____

③ **Task:** Read a book or article about a dinosaur. <u>State</u> what you learned on a separate piece of paper.

Name: _____

STATE *(cont.)*

☑ CHECK

Look back at what the word <u>state</u> means.

① Look at books about dinosaurs with classmates. 📝

② <u>State</u>, in writing, a fact you learned about dinosaurs. Use a separate piece of paper.

③ <u>State</u> your fact aloud and share it with classmates on an interactive whiteboard, flip chart, chart paper, or other message board.

④ Read and think about the facts your classmates shared. <u>State</u>, in writing, your opinion about dinosaurs based on what you have heard and read. Use the same separate piece of paper.

🔍 REVIEW

- We can <u>state</u> something by telling or explaining it in words.
- We can <u>state</u> information in writing.
- We can <u>state</u> what we think or believe about something.

💬 COLLABORATE

When we look back at what this word means, we see that it means to say or write something in words.

① <u>State</u> the name of a dinosaur to a classmate. Then <u>state</u> an interesting fact about that dinosaur.

② Ask your partner to <u>state</u> the name of a different dinosaur and an interesting fact about that dinosaur.

③ Take turns <u>stating</u> interesting facts about other dinosaurs. Write your facts on a separate piece of paper.

④ Work with your partner to rate the dinosaurs in order of most interesting to least interesting. Use the same separate piece of paper.

⑤ <u>State</u> your final opinion of the most interesting dinosaur and <u>state</u> why you think this.

_____

_____

_____

_____

Name: _____

COMPARE

 DEFINE

Question: What does it mean to <u>compare</u> two things or ideas?

Answer: When we <u>compare</u> two things or ideas, we judge them against each other. We look for how they are alike and different.

 STUDY

Sample Prompt: <u>Compare</u> a banana and an orange to show how they are alike and different.

Sample Answer: We peel both bananas and oranges before we eat them. Both are good fruits to pack in a lunch. They taste very different. An orange is juicy, and a banana is not juicy.

Sample Prompt: How would you <u>compare</u> the ways peaches and cantaloupe are alike?

Sample Answer: They are both sweet. The part we eat in each fruit is light orange.

✎ **PRACTICE**

① **Prompt:** <u>Compare</u> an apple and a pear. How are they alike? How are they different?

_____

_____

_____

_____

② **Prompt:** Look back at the two fruits you <u>compared</u> in Practice Prompt #1. Which do you like better? Why? Think about what each fruit is like to decide which is better.

_____

_____

_____

_____

③ **Prompt:** How do people <u>compare</u> different fruits? In what ways can fruits be compared?

_____

_____

_____

Name: _____

COMPARE *(cont.)*

☑ CHECK

Look back at what the word <u>compare</u> means.

① Work together with classmates to decide which two fruits you would like to <u>compare</u>.

② Share your thoughts and ideas as you and your classmates talk about how these fruits are alike and different.

③ Take part as the class creates a Venn diagram on an interactive whiteboard or chart paper to show how you have <u>compared</u> these fruits. [✐]

🔍 REVIEW

- When we <u>compare</u> two things, we think about how they are alike and different.
- Sometimes we <u>compare</u> two things we know are alike to show how they are alike.
- We can <u>compare</u> our answers to a question or prompt to classmates' answers to learn from each other.
- Sometimes when we <u>compare</u> two things, we decide which is better based on certain qualities.

💬 COLLABORATE

When we look back at what this word means, we see that it means to think about how two things are alike and different.

① Share your answers to Practice Prompts #1 and #2 with a partner.

② <u>Compare</u> your answers. How are they alike? How are they different?

_____

_____

③ Think about how your partner answered the prompts.

④ How did hearing what someone else thinks change your ideas about these fruits?

_____

_____

⑤ Write a new answer to the prompts to show how your ideas changed. Use a separate piece of paper.

Name: _____

CONTRAST

DEFINE

Question: What does it mean to <u>contrast</u> two things or ideas?
Answer: When we <u>contrast</u> two things or ideas, we name how they are different.

STUDY

Sample Prompt: <u>Contrast</u> the differences between a house and an apartment building.
Sample Answer: Only one family lives in a house. Many families live in an apartment building. Each family has their own apartment. Often, an apartment is smaller than a house. A house has a front door that goes outside. Sometimes, the front door to an apartment opens into a hallway.

Sample Prompt: <u>Contrast</u> the differences between a police station and a fire station.
Sample Answer: A fire station has fire trucks. Firefighters sometimes sleep at the fire station so they will be ready when there is a fire. There are police cars at the police station. The police do not stay overnight. They work a certain number of hours and then they go home.

✎ PRACTICE

① **Prompt:** <u>Contrast</u> a bookstore with a library.

_____

_____

_____

_____

_____

② **Prompt:** <u>Contrast</u> your house with your school.

_____

_____

_____

_____

_____

③ **Task:** Compare and <u>contrast</u> where you live (your house, apartment, etc.) in different seasons of the year. Draw pictures to show the differences on a separate piece of paper. Label your pictures.

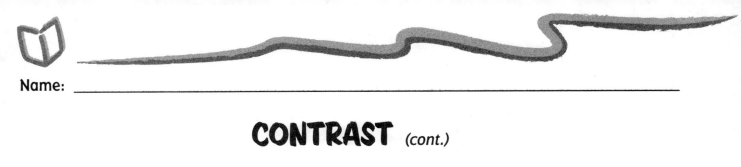

Name: _____

CONTRAST *(cont.)*

☑ CHECK

Look back at what the word <u>contrast</u> means.

① Write one or two sentences to <u>contrast</u> two buildings in your community. Use a separate piece of paper.

② Your teacher will ask you to share your ideas with the class. What <u>contrasts</u> in community buildings did your classmates share? Write your answer on the same piece of paper. 🖊️

③ Why is it important to <u>contrast</u> things and think about how they are different? Share your answer with the class.

🔍 REVIEW

- We <u>contrast</u> two things when we look closely to see how they are different.
- When we <u>contrast</u> two things, we point out and show how they are different.
- Sometimes, we <u>contrast</u> more than two things in a group.
- Often, when we <u>contrast</u> two things, we also compare them to see how they are alike.

💬 COLLABORATE

When we look back at what this word means, we see that it means to think about how two things are different.

① Write sentences about where you live.

_____

_____

_____

② Trade papers with a partner. Read your partner's sentences.

③ <u>Contrast</u> where you live with where your partner lives. How are these two places different?

_____

_____

_____

④ Talk about your answer with your partner.

Name: _____

DISCUSS

 DEFINE

Question: What does it mean to <u>discuss</u>?
Answer: When we <u>discuss</u>, we give our ideas and information about a topic. We can <u>discuss</u> a topic by talking or writing about it.

 STUDY

Sample Prompt: <u>Discuss</u> your ideas about how things in nature help people.
Sample Answer: People use plants for food. We need water to drink.

Sample Prompt: <u>Discuss</u> an experience you have had with plants. Think about reasons why plants help people.
Sample Answer: Our family planted a garden last summer. It was hard work because we had to water the plants. We also pulled weeds. The good part was we got healthy food to eat from the plants.

✎ **PRACTICE**

① **Prompt:** <u>Discuss</u> in writing how people use water as a natural resource.

_____

_____

_____

_____

② **Task:** <u>Discuss</u> how sunlight makes a difference in the way we live. What would our lives be like if we did not have sunlight? Write your ideas on the lines below. Leave "Your partner's ideas" blank for the Collaborate activity.

Your ideas: _____

_____

_____

Your partner's ideas: _____

_____

_____

③ **Task:** <u>Discuss</u> with classmates why you think people need air and water to live.

Name: _____

DISCUSS *(cont.)*

☑ CHECK

Look back at what the word <u>discuss</u> means.

① <u>Discuss</u> your answer to Practice Prompt #1 with a small group. On a separate piece of paper, take notes if needed to remember what your classmates say.

② <u>Discuss</u> ideas from your small group with the whole class. <u>Discuss</u> the topic by adding your thoughts to class notes on an interactive whiteboard or chart paper. Ask and answer questions about the topic to take part in the class-wide conversation. 📝

③ Think about how talking about a topic with classmates helps you learn. <u>Discuss</u> your ideas about how this helps you better understand and answer a writing prompt.

🔍 REVIEW

- We <u>discuss</u> a subject or an idea when we have a conversation about it with other people.
- When we <u>discuss</u> something, we might think about its good and bad points.
- We can <u>discuss</u> something by talking with others or writing about it.
  Example: We might <u>discuss</u> our ideas with a classmate by writing and sharing journal entries.
  Example: We can <u>discuss</u> ideas with classmates by adding our thoughts in writing to a whiteboard.

💬 COLLABORATE

When we look back at what this word means, we see that it means to talk with other people or write about the good and bad points about a subject.

A dialogue journal is a written conversation between two people.

① Trade the paper with your written answer to Practice Task #2 with a partner.

② Read your partner's answer to Practice Task #2. <u>Discuss</u> your thoughts about your partner's ideas by writing one or two sentences on the labeled lines.

③ Trade papers again. Read your partner's writing about your sentences.

④ <u>Discuss</u> with your partner the ideas and feedback you gave each other.

⑤ Continue to <u>discuss</u> the topic of how sunlight and other natural resources (soil, water, air) make a difference in the way we live.

Name: _____

GIVE AN EXAMPLE

DEFINE

Question: What does it mean to <u>give an example</u>?
Answer: When we <u>give an example</u>, we describe something typical of a larger group. An *example* may be a model for others to follow. It may also be a question or problem, along with a sample answer.

STUDY

Sample Prompt: <u>Give an example</u> of someone who helps other people in your community.
Sample Answer: A police officer helps our community by keeping people safe.

Sample Prompt: <u>Give an example</u> of how you can help people in your community.
Sample Answer: I can offer to help my neighbors water their flowers.

PRACTICE

① **Prompt:** <u>Give an example</u> of how people help each other in your community.

_____

_____

② **Task:** <u>Give an example</u> of a book you have read or heard read to you that tells something about the way people live together in a community.

_____

③ **Task:** <u>Give an example</u> of how people live in your city or town by drawing a picture.

GIVE AN EXAMPLE *(cont.)*

☑ CHECK

Look back at what it means to <u>give an example</u>.

① Work with a small group to plan how to <u>give an example</u> of how you could help someone in your community.

② Talk with your group about what you will include when you <u>give your example</u> to the class.

③ <u>Give your example</u> to other classmates by showing them your small group's work.

🔍 REVIEW

- We <u>give an example</u> when we describe one thing that is like the other things in a larger group.
- We can <u>give an example</u> for others to follow.
- We <u>give an example</u> when we show one way to answer a problem or question.

💬 COLLABORATE

When we look back at what this phrase means, we see that it means to describe how one thing is like other things in a group.

① Discuss your drawing in Practice Task #3 with a partner. How does your *example* show how people live in your city or town?

② What words could you add to your *example* to tell more about how people live in your town? Talk with your partner and take notes in the space below.

③ Look at your partner's response to Practice Task #2. Share the *example* you wrote. Then explain to your partner why this is a good *example*.

RESPOND

 ## DEFINE

Question: What does it mean to <u>respond</u>?
Answer: When we <u>respond</u>, we reply or give an answer. We say or write something in answer to a question.

 ## STUDY

Sample Prompt: <u>Respond</u> in writing to this prompt: What would it be like to run a race in the desert?
Sample Answer: A runner would have to carry lots of water and plan to run when the weather is not too hot.

Sample Prompt: Read the paragraph below. Then <u>respond</u> to the question.

Every year, runners race in Death Valley. One runner has an illness. One year, the sickness made her left side weak. She had to run with her arm in a sling. She found it was a good place to store an extra water bottle. This runner decided not to let illness stop her from reaching her goals.

How did the runner in Death Valley <u>respond</u> to her illness?

Sample Answer: She didn't let her illness stop her. When she had to wear a sling, she used it to carry extra water.

 ## PRACTICE

① **Prompt:** <u>Respond</u> in writing to the prompt: Would you want to run a race in the desert? Why or why not?

_____

_____

_____

② **Prompt:** How would you <u>respond</u> to this question: Why might a race in the desert begin at night?

_____

_____

③ **Prompt:** How would you <u>respond</u> if someone asked you to run in the desert with them?

_____

_____

RESPOND *(cont.)*

☑ CHECK

Look back at what the word <u>respond</u> means.

① Work with a small group to read information about people who take part in an extreme sport, or a sport that takes a lot of skill or strength.

② What would it be like if you did that sport? <u>Respond</u> in writing and then share your idea with the group.

_____

_____

_____

③ <u>Respond</u> as you ask and answer questions with your group about the sport.

🔍 REVIEW

- We <u>respond</u> when we reply or give an answer to someone.
- We can <u>respond</u> by reacting to something.
- When we <u>respond</u>, we say something in answer to something someone said or wrote.

💬 COLLABORATE

When we look back at what this word means, we see that it means to reply or give an answer to someone.

① <u>Respond</u> to what you have read and heard about extreme sports by writing questions you have.

_____

_____

_____

_____

_____

② Take turns sharing your questions with a partner.

③ <u>Respond</u> to your partner's questions by speaking aloud your answers.

Name: _____

RECALL

DEFINE

Question: What does it mean to <u>recall</u>?
Answer: When we <u>recall</u>, we remember something. We can <u>recall</u> an idea or an image in our mind.

STUDY

Sample Prompt: <u>Recall</u> a time when you saw someone ride a bicycle.
Sample Answer: I once saw a man in a rain jacket riding a bicycle.

Sample Prompt: <u>Recall</u> an experience you have had riding a bicycle.
Sample Answer: My family took a bicycle ride to the park and had a picnic.

PRACTICE

① **Prompt:** <u>Recall</u> a time when you wished you could ride a bicycle. Why did you want to ride it?

_____

_____

_____

② **Task:** <u>Recall</u> what a bicycle looks like. Draw a picture.

③ **Prompt:** <u>Recall</u> what you know about bicycles. Think about your own experience or what you have read or heard.

_____

_____

_____

RECALL *(cont.)*

☑ CHECK

Look back at what the word <u>recall</u> means.

① Talk with classmates to <u>recall</u> an interesting story you have heard or read about a bicycle.

② Work together to create a cartoon with different frames, or pictures, to show what happened in the story. Use a separate piece of paper.

③ <u>Recall</u> details about the story. Take turns sharing what makes this story interesting.

🔍 REVIEW

- When we <u>recall</u> something, we remember it.
- We can <u>recall</u> an idea or a picture and bring it to mind.
- We might <u>recall</u> something that happened in the past.

💬 COLLABORATE

When we look back at what this word means, we see that it means to tell about something that already happened.

① <u>Recall</u> what you know about bicycle safety.

② Use what you <u>recalled</u> to write questions for your partner about bicycle safety.

_____

_____

_____

_____

③ Trade papers with your partner.

④ <u>Recall</u> what you know about bicycle safety to answer your partner's questions.

_____

_____

_____

_____

EXAMINE

 ## DEFINE

Question: What does it mean to <u>examine</u> something?
Answer: When we <u>examine</u> something, we look carefully at it. We <u>examine</u> it to find out the facts about it.

 ## STUDY

Sample Prompt: <u>Examine</u> the paragraph below. Then answer the prompt.

> The head of a school in another country bought a plane. No one flew the plane anymore. He turned the plane into a classroom. Students could sit where the pilots sat. They could push buttons and pretend to fly the plane. They sat in chairs next to tables. The tables and chairs were lined up like seats in an airplane. Kids could look out the windows and pretend to fly anywhere in the world.

> What facts did you learn about this classroom from <u>examining</u> the paragraph?

Sample Answer: An old plane got turned into a classroom. Kids could sit in the cockpit and push the buttons as though they were flying the plane.

Sample Prompt: <u>Examine</u> your classroom by looking carefully around the room as you sit at your desk. Where do students sit? What things do you see in the classroom? What is on the walls of the room?
Sample Answer: This classroom has tables instead of desks. The shelves with supplies are easy to reach. There are a lot of windows.

 ## PRACTICE

① **Prompt:** <u>Examine</u> your classroom by looking carefully around the room as you sit at your desk. What facts about your classroom would a visitor find most interesting? Write what you noticed when you <u>examined</u> your classroom.

_____

_____

② **Task:** Read the paragraph below to <u>examine</u> information about a different kind of classroom. Write facts and other information you learned about the classroom.

Some students go to school outdoors for one week a year. They study plants and animals. They learn about soil and water. Students might go in the fall or in the spring. They stay in cabins at the outdoor school site.

_____

_____

EXAMINE *(cont.)*

☑ CHECK

Look back at what the word <u>examine</u> means.

① <u>Examine</u> your desk and classroom carefully again. Remember the details you notice.

② Take part in a beanbag-toss activity with classmates. When it is your turn, share one detail you noticed when you <u>examined</u> objects in your classroom. 📝

③ Then talk with classmates about your experience. What questions could you ask to <u>examine</u> your classroom in more detail? Here are two sample questions:

- What about our classroom makes learning fun?
- What would I like to see changed in our classroom?

🔍 REVIEW

- We <u>examine</u> something when we study it carefully to find out more about it.
- We can <u>examine</u> something by asking questions to learn more about it.
- When we look at something closely, we <u>examine</u> it.
- We might <u>examine</u> something to determine if it has any problems.

💬 COLLABORATE

When we look back at what this word means, we see that it means to study something carefully to find out more about it.

① You <u>examined</u> your classroom in Practice Prompt #1. What colors and types of pictures do you think should be in your classroom?

_____

_____

_____

_____

_____

_____

② Talk with a partner to <u>examine</u> ideas about different ways a classroom could look.

Name: _____

BRAINSTORM

DEFINE

Question: What does it mean to <u>brainstorm</u>?
Answer: When we <u>brainstorm</u>, we share ideas about a topic or how to solve a problem.

STUDY

Sample Prompt: <u>Brainstorm</u> what it would be like if plastic bags were banned in your town.
Sample Answer: Different things might happen. People would have to bring their own bags to the store. People might forget to bring bags. They would have to carry things in their arms. People wouldn't have plastic bags to use for their trash.

Sample Prompt: <u>Brainstorm</u> how things would be different if people had traveled in space a long time ago.
Sample Answer: In the past, people did not try to travel in space. They might have figured out a way to do it and put time and money into making it work. If people decided to travel in space a long time ago, they would not have worked on inventions to help people on Earth. We would not have all the technology on Earth that we do today.

PRACTICE

① **Prompt:** How do you <u>brainstorm</u> to get new ideas?

_____

_____

_____

② **Task:** Read the paragraph below about a current event. Then <u>brainstorm</u> how you would answer the questions. Write your ideas on the line below each question.

Many department stores are closing in towns. One reason may be that more people shop online. Some things cost less money online. But people may have to pay a fee to ship things to them. Online stores don't pay the same rent as stores in a mall. Things are stored in a large warehouse. Shoppers have more to choose from on a website.

How could this current event affect you and your family?

_____

How might this current event change the way people in your community live?

_____

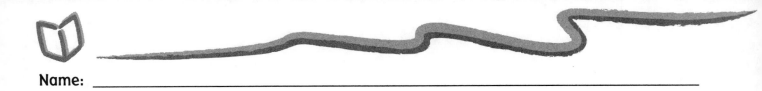

Name: _____

BRAINSTORM *(cont.)*

☑ CHECK

Look back at what the word <u>brainstorm</u> means.

① Work together with classmates to agree on a current problem in your town.

② Think about what you know about the problem.

③ Work together in a small group with other classmates who have knowledge and experience like yours.

④ How can people in your community solve the problem? <u>Brainstorm</u> your ideas and advice with your group. Write your group's ideas and advice in the boxes below.

Ideas	Advice

🔍 REVIEW

- When we <u>brainstorm</u>, we think of as many answers to a question or problem as possible.
- When we <u>brainstorm</u> with a group, we can write down or discuss everyone's ideas.
- We <u>brainstorm</u> to get new ideas and to help us plan.

💬 COLLABORATE

When we look back at what this word means, we see that it means to think of as many ideas as possible to answer a question.

① Review your notes from Practice Task #2.

② What in your family, community, or experience helped you think of your ideas?

Family: _____

Community: _____

Experience: _____

③ Share your ideas with a partner.

Name: _____

INTRODUCE

DEFINE

Question: What does it mean to <u>introduce</u> someone or something?
Answer: When we <u>introduce</u> someone or something, we let other people know about that person or thing. We give the name or tell something about the person or thing.

STUDY

Sample Prompt: <u>Introduce</u> the topic of your informative paragraph.
Sample Answer: A friend can help you do things.

Sample Prompt: How does an author <u>introduce</u> the main character of a story?
Sample Answer: An author tells readers the age of the character. Readers learn a little bit about the character. This helps readers care about what happens to the character.

✎ PRACTICE

① **Prompt:** What is something you think or believe about friends? Write a sentence to <u>introduce</u> your opinion about this topic.

_____

_____

② **Prompt:** Think of a topic about friends you might like to write about. How would you <u>introduce</u> your topic?

_____

_____

_____

_____

③ **Prompt:** Imagine you will write a story about friends. How would you <u>introduce</u> the main character in your story?

_____

_____

_____

_____

INTRODUCE (cont.)

☑ CHECK

Look back at what the word <u>introduce</u> means.

① Talk with classmates about a topic for an informative paragraph about friends.

② Write your ideas for key words to <u>introduce</u> the topic in the box below.

③ <u>Introduce</u> the topic in a sentence.

_____

_____

_____

④ Share your sentence with classmates. Talk about how your sentence <u>introduces</u> the topic.

🔍 REVIEW

- When we <u>introduce</u> something, we might say something new about it.
- We <u>introduce</u> something when we make something known by name.
- We can <u>introduce</u> something for people to think about or discuss.
- When we <u>introduce</u> something, we say or write about it for the first time.

💬 COLLABORATE

When we look back at what this word means, we see that it means to let other people know about something by naming it or saying something new about it.

① What questions could you ask a classmate to help <u>introduce</u> him or her to someone else? Write the questions on a separate piece of paper.

② Ask your partner the questions you wrote to help <u>introduce</u> him or her. Write what your partner says on the same separate piece of paper.

③ Use your notes to <u>introduce</u> your partner to the class.

Name: _____

ORDER

DEFINE

Question: What does it mean to <u>order</u> things or events?
Answer: When we <u>order</u> things or events, we write or place them in a certain way.

STUDY

Sample Prompt: How would you <u>order</u> the events in your life this week?
Sample Answer: I would group events by what happened yesterday, today, and tomorrow.

Sample Prompt: Describe how you <u>order</u> the events in your morning.
Sample Answer: First, I get dressed. Then I eat breakfast. Finally, I brush my teeth and comb my hair.

✏️ PRACTICE

① **Prompt:** How do you <u>order</u> the activities you will do after school?

_____

_____

_____

_____

② **Prompt:** How would you <u>order</u> the events that happened today to tell an interesting story?

_____

_____

_____

_____

③ **Prompt:** How would you <u>order</u> events in your life to make a perfect day?

_____

_____

_____

_____

Name: _____

ORDER *(cont.)*

☑ CHECK

Look back at what the word <u>order</u> means.

  ① Which "time" words help us <u>order</u> events in our writing?

  ② With a small group, add more "time" words to the chart below.

  ③ Share your ideas with the whole class.

  ④ Fill in the rest of the chart with your classmates' ideas.

Time Words		
first		
then		
finally		

🔍 REVIEW

- When we <u>order</u> things or events, we list them in a certain way.
- We arrange things when we <u>order</u> them.
  Example: We <u>order</u> numbers from smallest to largest.
  Example: We might <u>order</u> words by the first letter using the order of the alphabet.

💬 COLLABORATE

When we look back at what this word means, we see that it means to list things or events in a certain way.

  ① Review your answer to Practice Prompt #3.

  ② Share your ideas with a classmate.

  ③ Work together to <u>order</u> events that would happen in a story about a perfect day.

  ④ Help each other include time words from the chart above to <u>order</u> the events in your story.

  ⑤ Share your story with other classmates.

DEMONSTRATE

DEFINE

Question: What does it mean to <u>demonstrate</u>?

Answer: When we <u>demonstrate</u>, we show that we know or understand something. We do something to show it clearly.

STUDY

Sample Task: <u>Demonstrate</u> your understanding of the story by circling key details.

A school bus company studied safety. It learned that students are safer on a school bus than they are in a car. School buses are yellow because that color stands out. The black letters are easy to read. Everyone knows a school bus has children on board.

Sample Answer: A (school bus) company studied (safety). It learned that students are safer on a school bus than they are in (a car). School buses are (yellow) because that color stands out. The (black letters) are easy to read. Everyone knows a school bus has (children) on board.

Sample Prompt: <u>Demonstrate</u> what you know about school buses by writing a sentence.

Sample Answer: About half of the students in my school ride the school bus.

PRACTICE

① **Task:** Read the paragraph. <u>Demonstrate</u> your understanding of what you read by answering the questions below.

We often see yellow school buses. In some places, school buses may be other colors. One school bus is yellow because it looks like a cartoon character. In a village on an island, students take a boat to school. What color do you think the boat is? If you guessed "yellow," you are right!

What color are many school buses?

_____

What different types of school buses does the paragraph talk about?

_____

_____

② **Prompt:** Where do school buses take people? <u>Demonstrate</u> your understanding of school buses by writing a few sentences on a separate piece of paper.

DEMONSTRATE (cont.)

☑ CHECK

Look back at what the word demonstrate means.

① What do you know about how kids should act on a school bus? Demonstrate what you know by writing your answer on the lines.

_____

_____

_____

_____

② Share your answer with classmates in a small group.

③ Discuss every idea shared.

④ Practice a role-play to demonstrate your ideas to other classmates.

⑤ Present your role-play to the class.

⌕ REVIEW

- We can demonstrate that we understand something by showing clearly what we know.
- We can demonstrate a task to show other people how to do something.
- We can demonstrate our understanding by asking and answering questions.

💬 COLLABORATE

When we look back at what this word means, we see that it means to do something to show that we understand what we read or hear about a subject.

① Think about what you noticed when classmates demonstrated their ideas about how students should act on a school bus.

② How well did your classmates demonstrate what they knew about the topic?

③ Talk with a partner about how each group demonstrated its understanding of how to act on a school bus.

④ Work with your partner to complete a web on a separate piece of paper. Write ways your classmates demonstrated their knowledge in the bubbles on the web.

Name: _____

PARTICIPATE

DEFINE

Question: What does it mean to <u>participate</u>?

Answer: When we <u>participate</u>, we join with others in an activity or event.

STUDY

Sample Prompt: How can you <u>participate</u> in a conversation?

Sample Answer: I can take turns listening to others and sharing my thoughts about a subject.

Sample Prompt: How did Javier and Ava <u>participate</u> in an activity at a theme park?

Sample Answer: They <u>participated</u> in an activity by climbing to the top of a water slide and then going down the slide together on a plastic mat.

✏️ PRACTICE

① **Prompt:** How do you think Mr. Walt Disney <u>participated</u> in building Disneyland?

_____

_____

_____

_____

② **Prompt:** What would be your favorite thing to <u>participate</u> in at a theme park like Disneyland?

_____

_____

_____

_____

③ **Prompt:** How could you <u>participate</u> in planning something fun for your friends or family?

_____

_____

_____

_____

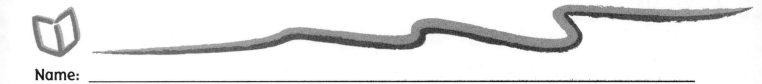

Name: _____

PARTICIPATE (cont.)

☑ CHECK

Look back at what the word <u>participate</u> means.

<u>Participate</u> with a small group to describe a ride or other feature you would like to see added to a theme park. Complete the chart with your group members.

Questions to Think About	Group Ideas
What would be the name of the ride or feature?	
What would the ride or feature look like?	
What would the ride or feature do?	
What would make the ride or feature different and fun?	

🔍 REVIEW

- When we <u>participate</u> in something, we share it in common with other people.
- We connect with others when we <u>participate</u> in doing something together.
- We can <u>participate</u> by taking part in an activity with other people.

💬 COLLABORATE

When we look back at what this word means, we see that it means to join with others to do something.

① Read the questions below. Think about how you <u>participated</u> with a small group during the Check activity. Take notes on a separate piece of paper.

- What did you share in common with classmates when you <u>participated</u> in the small-group activity?
- How did you connect with others to do something together?
- How did you take part in the small-group activity?

② Talk with a classmate who was not part of your small group during the Check activity.

③ <u>Participate</u> in a conversation with your partner to share your answers to the questions listed above.

Name: _____

PREDICT

 DEFINE

Question: What does it mean to <u>predict</u> something?

Answer: When we <u>predict</u> something, we say what we think will happen in the future.

 STUDY

Sample Prompt: If a person in a story saw a large sea monster, what do you <u>predict</u> would happen next in the story?

Sample Answer: The person might go tell everyone in town. Maybe the people in the town would try to catch the sea monster. Or maybe they would all be afraid and move to another place.

Sample Prompt: What do you <u>predict</u> a dragon would do in a story?

Sample Answer: A dragon might carry people out of danger.

✏️ **PRACTICE**

① **Task:** Read the story starter below. What do you <u>predict</u> will happen next in the story?

I stopped climbing to catch my breath. As I looked across the valley, a unicorn came up the trail. Quickly, I hid behind a rock so I wouldn't scare it away. The splendid animal held its head up. It sniffed the air and then stepped around a tree toward a pond. The forest grew very still. I imagined all the animals held their breath, waiting to see what the unicorn would do.

_____

_____

_____

_____

② **Prompt:** Imagine that a mythical creature lived today. What do you <u>predict</u> would happen to that creature if it lived in your community?

_____

_____

_____

_____

_____

PREDICT *(cont.)*

☑ CHECK

Look back at what the word <u>predict</u> means.

① Your teacher will display a picture of a mythical creature. Look at the picture. 📝

② What do you <u>predict</u> would happen in a story about this creature? Take notes about your ideas.

_____

_____

_____

_____

_____

③ Work with a small group to write a story together about this creature. Use a separate piece of paper.

🔍 REVIEW

- We <u>predict</u> something when we tell what we think will happen in the future.
- When we <u>predict</u>, we look at what has already happened to say what we think will happen next.
- We can use our experience and what we know to help us <u>predict</u> what will happen next.

💬 COLLABORATE

When we look back at what this word means, we see that it means to say what we think will happen in the future.

Use a separate piece of paper to complete the following tasks:

① Read a classmate's answer to Practice Prompt #2. What did he or she <u>predict</u> would happen to the mythical creature?

② What questions could you ask to <u>predict</u> what happens next in the story he or she might write?

③ With your partner, review the questions above. How do his or her questions help you better <u>predict</u> what might happen in a story?

④ Work together with your partner to use your ideas about what you both <u>predict</u> would happen to write a story about a mythical creature in your community.

Name: _____

CONNECT

 DEFINE

Question: What does it mean to <u>connect</u> two things (in writing)?

Answer: When we <u>connect</u> two things, we show how they go together. In writing, we might use a certain word to show that two things go together. This word might be *also*, *because*, or *so*. We can <u>connect</u> what we think (*an opinion*) with why we think that (*our reason*). We might write a sentence to explain how two things, ideas, people, or events go together.

 STUDY

Sample Prompt: Write a sentence that <u>connects</u> two ideas.

Sample Answer: I swim every day, so I exercise often.

Sample Prompt: Write a sentence that <u>connects</u> an opinion (*what you think*) with a reason (*why you think this*).

Sample Answer: Baseball is the best sport because players get to do more than one thing.

✎ **PRACTICE**

① **Prompt:** What is your opinion about running? Write a sentence to <u>connect</u> your opinion with one reason why you think this.

_____

_____

② **Task:** Read the paragraph below. Underline the sentence that tells the author's opinion. Circle the word that <u>connects</u> a reason with the opinion.

Soccer is a great game because it can be played all year. In the fall, the air is crisp and cool. When the sun shines, the best place to be is on the soccer field. Some places have indoor soccer. People can play inside during bad winter weather. In the spring, the weather gets warm again. The days are perfect for running outside with a soccer ball. It is also a game kids play for fun or in soccer matches for points. For these reasons, soccer is my favorite game!

③ **Prompt:** Write a sentence to show a <u>connection</u> between basketball and volleyball. How do the two sports go together?

_____

_____

_____

CONNECT *(cont.)*

☑ CHECK

Look back at what the word <u>connect</u> means.

① On a separate slip of paper, copy the sentence you wrote for Practice Prompt #1.

② Do not write your name on the slip of paper. Your teacher will collect the anonymous sentences and read them. 📝

③ Listen to the sentences your classmates wrote.

④ Give a thumbs-up or thumbs-down signal to show which sentences <u>connect</u> an opinion to a reason in a way that makes sense.

🔍 REVIEW

- We can <u>connect</u> two ideas.
- We can <u>connect</u> an opinion with a reason for the opinion.
- We can <u>connect</u> one person to another.
  Examples: characters in a narrative, historical figures
- We can <u>connect</u> one event to another.
  Examples: events in a narrative, historical events, events in nature

💬 COLLABORATE

When we look back at what this word means, we see that it means to show how two things go together.

① How can you <u>connect</u> what you know about one sport to another sport?

_____

_____

_____

_____

② Work with a classmate to create a Venn diagram to show how you <u>connected</u> one sport to another sport. Use a separate piece of paper.

③ Rehearse with your partner how you would explain how you <u>connected</u> your ideas about two different sports. How would you explain your diagram to a family member?

Name: _____

CONCLUDE/DRAW A CONCLUSION

 DEFINE

Question: What does it mean to <u>conclude</u>? How do we <u>draw a conclusion</u>?
Answer: When we <u>conclude</u> something, we finish it. When we <u>draw a conclusion</u>, we use facts to make a decision. We might realize something based on those facts.

 STUDY

Sample Prompt: From what you have heard or read, what do you <u>conclude</u> about people traveling to Mars in the future?
Sample Answer: We have experience in space travel. Our knowledge will help people go to Mars one day.

Sample Prompt: How would you <u>conclude</u> a paragraph with this topic sentence?
   No other planets in our solar system are exactly like Earth.

Sample Answer: We live on a wonderful and special planet!

 PRACTICE

① **Task:** Read the fact cards. Then write a *concluding* sentence for each card. Use a separate piece of paper.

> **Fact Card #1**
> There is a research station in space. It is called the International Space Station. People from different countries work and live there. Some crew members go on space walks. They do work on the station to keep everything running the way it should.

> **Fact Card #2**
> A spacecraft was sent to Jupiter. It orbited the planet for two years. The mission studied the atmosphere of the planet. It also looked closely at the north and south poles.

② **Task:** Read the paragraph below. Then write one or more sentences to <u>conclude</u> the paragraph. Use the same separate piece of paper.

Astronauts are people who travel to outer space. They have to meet certain requirements. Some people who go into space have a lot of experience as pilots. Other people have special training. Some go into the space program from the military. All astronauts must pass a test to make sure they are healthy. They also answer personal questions to show they can work with others in space.

③ **Prompt:** Think about what you have read. What do you <u>conclude</u> about outer space?

_____

_____

CONCLUDE/DRAW A CONCLUSION *(cont.)*

☑ CHECK

Look back at what the word <u>conclude</u> means. Think about what it means to <u>conclude</u> something or to <u>draw a conclusion</u>.

① Discuss with classmates what it means to <u>conclude</u> a paragraph or topic.

② Your teacher will display a sample paragraph that has a *concluding* sentence. 📝

③ As a class, discuss the questions below to decide how well the author <u>concluded</u> the paragraph.

- How did the author restate the topic using different words?
- How did the author review the main ideas in the paragraph?
- How did the author use facts and reasons to <u>conclude</u> his or her thoughts?

🔍 REVIEW

- When we <u>conclude</u> something, we bring it to an end. We finish it.
- We <u>draw a conclusion</u> when we decide something using facts or reasons.
- We can <u>conclude</u> something based on the facts.
- We can <u>conclude</u> something by restating the topic in different words.

💬 COLLABORATE

When we look back at what this word means, we see that it means to use facts and reasons to decide something or provide a final sentence.

① Talk with a partner about what it means to <u>conclude</u> something or <u>draw a conclusion</u>.

② Complete the chart below to practice <u>drawing a conclusion</u> about space travel.

What facts do you know about space travel?	
What have you decided about space travel based on those facts?	
What are your reasons for making this decision?	

③ Work together to write a sentence that <u>concludes</u> your thoughts about space travel.

_____

_____

Name: _____

SELECT

 DEFINE

Question: What does it mean to <u>select</u> something?
Answer: When we <u>select</u> something, we pick it out or choose it.

 STUDY

Sample Task: <u>Select</u> the answer that best describes a biome.

  a. a glass bubble

  b. a certain environment where plants and animals live

  c. the ocean

  d. the connection between plants and animals and where they live

Sample Answer: The correct answer is b. A biome is a certain environment where plants and animals live.

Sample Task: <u>Select</u> the correct answer from the answer choices below.

Which biome has mostly grass and flowers with only a few trees?

  a. rainforest   b. desert   c. grassland   d. woodland

Sample Answer: c. grassland

 PRACTICE

① **Task:** Read the paragraph below. Then read the question. <u>Select</u> the correct answer from the answer choices.

The tundra is very cold. Not many plants grow there. Even though it is cold, it does not rain or snow very much. There is about a month of summer when it gets warm enough for plants to grow. Certain animals also live in the tundra. They have ways to survive in the cold weather.

Which word best describes the tundra biome?

  a. wet   b. forest   c. warm   d. cold

② **Task:** <u>Select</u> which biome you would most like to visit by drawing a circle around its name. Write one or two sentences to tell why you would like to visit this place.

> forest   desert   coast   grassland

_____

_____

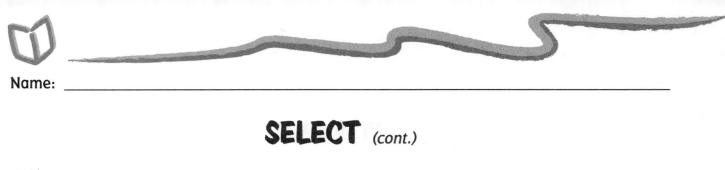

SELECT (cont.)

☑ CHECK

Look back at what the word <u>select</u> means.

① Look at the pictures of biomes your teacher shows the class. 🖊

② <u>Select</u> the picture that shows a rainforest biome. How did you know which picture to <u>select</u>? Discuss as a class.

③ <u>Select</u> a picture that shows the type of environment in which you live. Talk with classmates about your answer.

🔍 REVIEW

- We <u>select</u> something by choosing it.
- When we <u>select</u> something, we choose it from a group.
- When we <u>select</u> something, we choose it because it is the best fit.
- On a computer, we <u>select</u> words or an action by using a mouse to highlight it.

💬 COLLABORATE

When we look back at what this word means, we see that it means to choose something from a group of things or actions.

① <u>Select</u> an activity you would like to do to tell others about your favorite biome.
   a. Draw a picture.
   b. Read about it and write sentences.
   c. Make a page to display on a computer or interactive whiteboard.
   d. Make a poster.

② With a partner, <u>select</u> one biome you will learn about together. <u>Select</u> one or more ways to learn about this biome.
   a. Read a book.
   b. Look at pictures.
   c. Look at a website.
   d. Talk to someone who knows about the subject.

③ Take notes about what you learn.

_____

_____

Name: _____

ESTIMATE

 DEFINE

Question: What does it mean to <u>estimate</u>?
Answer: When we <u>estimate</u>, we make a reasonable guess about something. After we <u>estimate</u>, we can check to see if we are right by counting or measuring the actual amount.

 STUDY

Sample Prompt: <u>Estimate</u> the length of the whiteboard at the front of the classroom.
Sample Answer: I think the whiteboard is seven or eight feet long.

Sample Prompt: <u>Estimate</u> how long it will take your class to line up for lunch.
Sample Answer: I think it will take us five minutes to line up for lunch.

 PRACTICE

① **Prompt:** <u>Estimate</u> the length of your math book in inches. _____

What is the actual length of your math book? How closely did you <u>estimate</u> the length?

_____

_____

② **Prompt:** <u>Estimate</u> how many leaf shapes you can cut out of a piece of green paper. Then tell how you could check to see if you <u>estimated</u> correctly.

_____

_____

_____

③ **Prompt:** How long do you <u>estimate</u> your set of watercolor paints will last? What would make a difference in how long you will be able to use the paints?

_____

_____

_____

_____

ESTIMATE *(cont.)*

☑ CHECK

Look back at what the word <u>estimate</u> means.

① Think of a time when you <u>estimated</u> the size or value of something. How did you use what you already know to help you <u>estimate</u>?

② Share your experience with classmates in a small group.

③ Work together as a group to create a poster to help others think about how to <u>estimate</u> different things.

🔍 REVIEW

- When we <u>estimate</u>, we guess the size or value of something.
- We can <u>estimate</u> how much of something we will need to complete a task.
- We use our past experiences to <u>estimate</u>.
- We <u>estimate</u> when we form an opinion about how large or small something is.

💬 COLLABORATE

When we look back at what this word means, we see that it means to guess the size or value of something.

① How can we <u>estimate</u> to help us solve a problem?

_____

_____

_____

② Talk with a partner about your answer to the question above.

③ Talk with your partner about how <u>estimating</u> would help you in the real-world task in Practice Prompt #2.

④ Think together about how you could <u>estimate</u> to complete a task this week in the classroom. Write your ideas below.

_____

_____

_____

MATCH

 DEFINE

Question: What does it mean to <u>match</u> things?

Answer: When we <u>match</u> things, we put together things that go well with each other.

 STUDY

Sample Task: Read the sentence and words below. <u>Match</u> the toy or item that the children in the sentence might play with by circling the correct answer.

Ethan and Madison like to pretend they are fighting a dragon to save the kingdom.

Sample Answer:

basketball   colored markers   doll   fire truck   (knight and castle playset)

Sample Task: Which toys or items would kids play with outside? Which toys or items would they use inside? <u>Match</u> each toy or item to the place where kids would play with it. Write the name of each toy or item in the correct box below.

sidewalk chalk   modeling clay   video game   bubble wand

Sample Answer:

Outside	**Inside**
sidewalk chalk	modeling clay
bubble wand	video game

 PRACTICE

① **Task:** Which items go together? Write each action word next to each <u>matching</u> toy or item.

jump   throw   kick   draw

pogo stick: _____   sidewalk chalk: _____

soccer ball: _____   flying disc: _____

② **Task:** <u>Match</u> each toy or item to a related toy or item. Draw lines to connect the toys or items that go together.

model cars	helmet
baseball	play mat
building-block set	bat
scooter	racetrack

MATCH (cont.)

✓ CHECK

① Draw a picture of your favorite toy.

② Display it on a bulletin board with your classmates' drawings.

③ Which of your classmates' toys <u>match</u> your toy? Draw lines or use string to <u>match</u> the toy in your drawing to the pictures of your classmates' toys that go with it.

○ REVIEW

· We <u>match</u> two or more things that go well together.

· When we <u>match</u> two or more things, we find things that are similar.

💬 COLLABORATE

When we look back at what this word means, we see that it means to put things together that are alike.

① Look back at the sample tasks and the practice tasks on page 76. Then think about how you and your classmates <u>matched</u> toys in the Check activity above.

② Think of three toys. Write them on the lines on the left. Write one or more clues for each toy. Write them out of order on the lines on the right.

_____   _____

                               _____

_____   _____

                               _____

_____   _____

                               _____

③ Share your clues with a partner. Ask him or her to <u>match</u> each clue with the correct toy.

Name: _____

CONVINCE

 DEFINE

Question: What does it mean to <u>convince</u> someone?
Answer: When we <u>convince</u> someone, we make someone believe what we say.

 STUDY

Sample Prompt: Write a sentence to <u>convince</u> someone that board games are fun to play.
Sample Answer: Board games are fun to play because you can talk to your friends while you play.

Sample Prompt: What would you say to <u>convince</u> someone that tag is the best outdoor game?
Sample Answer: Tag is the best outdoor game to play because lots of people can play at the same time.

✏️ **PRACTICE**

① **Prompt:** What is your favorite game? Write a sentence to <u>convince</u> someone that this is a great game.

_____

_____

② **Prompt:** Why do you like this game? Write reasons that will <u>convince</u> classmates to try playing your favorite game.

_____

_____

_____

_____

③ **Prompt:** What facts do you know that you could add to your reasons to <u>convince</u> someone to play this game?

_____

_____

_____

_____

CONVINCE *(cont.)*

☑ CHECK

Look back at what the word <u>convince</u> means.

① Talk with classmates to agree on a game that many people like to play.

② On a separate piece of paper, write reasons to <u>convince</u> others that this is a fun game to play. Do not write your names on your paper. Turn in your paper to your teacher. 🖉

③ Your teacher will display the reasons you and your classmates wrote.

④ Take turns using a student response system with the interactive whiteboard to mark the reasons that help <u>convince</u> you to try playing this game. Or, if the reasons are displayed on a bulletin board, take turns writing check marks next to the reasons that <u>convinced</u> you.

⑤ Talk about how these reasons <u>convince</u> you that this is a fun game.

🔍 REVIEW

· We <u>convince</u> someone when we make them believe something is true.

· We can <u>convince</u> someone to agree to do something.

· We use reasons and facts to <u>convince</u> someone to believe what we say.

💬 COLLABORATE

When we look back at what this word means, we see that it means to use facts and reasons to make someone believe something.

① Talk about your answers to the practice prompts with a partner.

② Think about your classmate's answer to each prompt. Which reasons and facts helped <u>convince</u> you to agree with your partner?

③ Complete the chart below. If a reason <u>convinced</u> you to agree with your classmate, write the reason in the left column. If a reason needs more work to <u>convince</u> you, write the reason in the right column. Discuss your answers with your partner.

	This reason <u>convinced</u> me to agree this game is fun.	Let's work on this reason together so people will be more <u>convinced</u> this is a good game.
Practice Prompt #1		
Practice Prompt #2		
Practice Prompt #3		

LIST

📖 DEFINE

Question: What does it mean to <u>list</u> things?
Answer: When we <u>list</u> things, we write them in a series.

📖 STUDY

Sample Prompt: <u>List</u> the types of buses people can ride.
Sample Answer: People can ride a school bus, city bus, or tour bus.

Sample Prompt: <u>List</u> different types of boats in alphabetical order.
Sample Answer: Some different types of boats are canoes, kayaks, row boats, sailboats, and yachts.

✏️ PRACTICE

① **Prompt:** <u>List</u> the different ways people can travel.

_____

_____

② **Task:** <u>List</u> the ways you travel in the order of the way you travel most often.

_____

_____

③ **Task:** Think about a story you could write about one way people travel. <u>List</u> your ideas for the story in the chart below. Then write your story on a separate piece of paper.

Story topic	
Characters	
Where the story takes place	
What happens	
How the story ends	

Name: _____

LIST *(cont.)*

☑ CHECK

Look back at what the word <u>list</u> means.

① Work with classmates to <u>list</u> what you **know** about ways people travel in the first column of a K-W-H-L chart. Use a separate piece of paper.

② Discuss and <u>list</u> in the second column of the chart **what** you would like to learn about how people travel.

③ **How** could you learn this new information? In the third column of the chart, <u>list</u> ways you and your classmates could discover what you want to know.

④ Work with a small group to read about ways people travel. Ask each other questions to learn new information from each other about one or more ways people travel. [!]

⑤ <u>List</u> the new information you **learned** in the last column to complete the chart.

○ REVIEW

- Often we will <u>list</u> a series of names or things in a certain order.
- We might <u>list</u> reasons to tell someone why we feel a certain way about something.
- When we think about a topic before we write, we might <u>list</u> our ideas.

⌨ COLLABORATE

When we look back at what this word means, we see that it means to write a series of names or things, often in a certain order.

Complete the following tasks on a separate piece of paper:

① Think about your favorite way to travel. <u>List</u> reasons why you like this way of travel best.

② Compare the type of travel you described to a classmate's choice of travel. Which reasons apply to both ways of travel?

③ Work with your partner to <u>list</u> reasons people choose one way of travel over another way.

④ Which of the reasons you <u>listed</u> for #3 might be the most important? <u>List</u> the reasons you and your partner discussed in order from most important to least important.

Name: _____

INFORM

 DEFINE

Question: What does it mean to <u>inform</u>?
Answer: When we <u>inform</u>, we tell someone something. We might use facts and information to <u>inform</u> readers about a topic.

 STUDY

Sample Prompt: How would a teacher <u>inform</u> parents about a class trip to the zoo?
Sample Answer: The teacher could write a letter to the parents.

Sample Prompt: How would you <u>inform</u> readers about the topic of wild animals in parks?
Sample Answer: I would read about this kind of park to learn about it. Then I would write the most interesting facts and information in my own words.

✎ **PRACTICE**

① **Prompt:** What is your favorite kind of wildlife? What would you tell someone to <u>inform</u> them about this type of wildlife?

_____

_____

② **Prompt:** Think of a topic about wild animals. How would you <u>inform</u> readers about your topic? Write a paragraph to <u>inform</u> people about your topic. Use a separate piece of paper.

③ **Task:** Read the paragraph below. Then answer the question.

Wild animals find their own food. They do not rely on people to take care of them. They live in the wild, separate from people. Some wild animals live in captivity. This means people have caught them. These animals live in a zoo or in a park. People feed animals in a zoo, but the animals are not tame. A tame animal is usually not dangerous to people.

What facts and information does the author give to <u>inform</u> readers about the topic?

_____

_____

_____

_____

Name: _____

INFORM *(cont.)*

☑ CHECK

Look back at what the word <u>inform</u> means.

① In a small group, decide on a topic about wild animals.

② Work together to gather information about the topic.

③ Decide with your group how you will <u>inform</u> classmates about what you learned. Take notes in the box below.

┌───┐
│   │
│   │
│   │
│   │
└───┘

④ Share with the class to <u>inform</u> them about your topic.

🔍 REVIEW

- When we give information about someone or something, we <u>inform</u>.
- We <u>inform</u> someone when we tell them one or more facts about something.
- We <u>inform</u> when we share something about a topic.

💬 COLLABORATE

When we look back at what this word means, we see that it means to give information to let a person know about something.

① How would you <u>inform</u> someone about the zoo?

_____

_____

_____

_____

② Share your answer with a partner.

③ Work together to create a booklet with pictures to <u>inform</u> readers about this topic.

Name: _____

EVALUATE

DEFINE

Question: What does it mean to <u>evaluate</u>?
Answer: When we <u>evaluate</u>, we think carefully about something to decide how good or valuable it is. We decide why something is important.

STUDY

Sample Prompt: <u>Evaluate</u> why superheroes are popular.
Sample Answer: People want good to win over evil. People also like the idea of someone having special powers.

Sample Prompt: How would you <u>evaluate</u> a superhero to decide if he or she is important?
Sample Answer: I would <u>evaluate</u> a superhero by looking at what the character does and says. I would see if he or she helps people, does good things, or has superpowers.

✏️ PRACTICE

① **Prompt:** <u>Evaluate</u> your favorite superhero. Why might people like this hero? What good traits does he or she have?

_____

_____

_____

② **Prompt:** What do we learn from superheroes? <u>Evaluate</u> how reading about a superhero might help other kids.

_____

_____

③ **Task:** Read the story below. <u>Evaluate</u> the role the superhero character plays. How is he important to the story?

Super Turtle walked along the road. He did not run, but he kept a steady pace. He knew he would win the race. Rabbit flew by in a flash of fur. Rabbit ran so fast, he did not see Sheep Dog by the side of the road. Sheep Dog lay in the grass. Super Turtle stopped to see why Sheep Dog was not running in the race. Sheep Dog had a thorn in his paw. Super Turtle stopped to help him take it out.

_____

EVALUATE *(cont.)*

☑ CHECK

Look back at what the word <u>evaluate</u> means.

① Look at the comic strip your teacher displays. 🖊

② Who is the superhero character? What does this character say and do?

_____

_____

_____

③ In the right-hand boxes, draw your own version of what this character might say and do. <u>Evaluate</u> what you need to have in your drawing to show why this superhero is important.

④ Share your drawings with your classmates.

1

2

3

🔍 REVIEW

- When we <u>evaluate</u>, we determine the worth or value of something.
- We <u>evaluate</u> something when we determine how important it is.
- We study something carefully to <u>evaluate</u> its worth or value.

💬 COLLABORATE

When we look back at what this word means, we see that it means to determine how important or valuable something is.

① <u>Evaluate</u> a classmate's answer to Practice Prompt #1. How does he or she show the value or worth of a superhero character?

_____

_____

_____

② Share with your partner the drawings you made in Check #3. <u>Evaluate</u> and discuss how well you each did at showing why superheroes are important.

Name: _____

ILLUSTRATE

 ## DEFINE

Question: What does it mean to <u>illustrate</u> something?
Answer: When we <u>illustrate</u> something, we create real or mental pictures. We use words or pictures as examples to explain something or make something easy to understand.

 ## STUDY

Sample Prompt: Which shape would best <u>illustrate</u> a hardware store?

 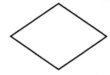 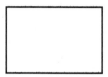

Sample Answer: The rectangle <u>illustrates</u> a hardware store. Many hardware stores are in the shape of a rectangle.

Sample Prompt: What words or pictures would you use to <u>illustrate</u> a grocery store?
Sample Answer: I would <u>illustrate</u> a grocery store with the words *store*, *food*, *fruit*, *vegetables*, and *sale signs*. I could draw pictures of the food or people with carts to <u>illustrate</u> the store.

 ## PRACTICE

① **Prompt:** What words would you use to <u>illustrate</u> your favorite clothing store?

_____

_____

_____

② **Task:** Create pictures to <u>illustrate</u> pets you might find at a pet store.

ILLUSTRATE *(cont.)*

☑ CHECK

Look back at what the word <u>illustrate</u> means.

① Listen as your teacher reads a story. He or she will not show you the pictures. [!]

② How would you <u>illustrate</u> the story? Think about the people, places, things, and actions described in the story.

③ On a separate piece of paper, draw pictures to <u>illustrate</u> the main parts of the story. Color the pictures.

④ Share your pictures with your classmates.

🔍 REVIEW

- When we <u>illustrate</u> something, we explain it to make it clear.
- We can give an example to <u>illustrate</u> something to make it easy to understand.
- We can <u>illustrate</u> something by adding pictures or drawings to our writing.
- When we <u>illustrate</u> our writing with pictures, it can explain or decorate our writing.

💬 COLLABORATE

When we look back at what this word means, we see that it means to use words or pictures to make something easy to understand.

① Write words or sentences to describe a store you like to go to with your family. Use a separate piece of paper.

② Take turns reading your words to a partner.

③ Draw a picture to <u>illustrate</u> the type of store your partner described.

④ Check with your partner to see how well your drawings <u>illustrated</u> the store he or she has visited.

SEQUENCE

 DEFINE

Question: What does it mean to <u>sequence</u> things?
Answer: When we <u>sequence</u> things, we place them in a certain order.

 STUDY

Sample Prompt: Why do we <u>sequence</u> events that happen in order?
Sample Answer: It makes it easy to know what happens first, next, and last.

Sample Prompt: <u>Sequence</u> these events that might happen at a family picnic.

- hike
- swim
- sit on a blanket
- take a nap
- play catch
- eat

Sample Answer: First, we might take a hike around the park. Then we might eat a picnic lunch. Next, some of us might play catch. Then we might go swimming. After that, we might sit on a blanket to dry off. Finally, we might take a nap.

 PRACTICE

① **Task:** <u>Sequence</u> the events listed below for a family story. Which event might happen at the beginning of the story? the middle? the end?

> picnic   music in the park   parade   fireworks   egg-toss game   water-balloon fun

1. _____   4. _____

2. _____   5. _____

3. _____   6. _____

② **Task:** Think of a holiday or special day you and your family celebrate. <u>Sequence</u> the things you do to celebrate. Use a separate piece of paper.

③ **Task:** Read the story events listed below. <u>Sequence</u> the events to write your own story on a separate piece of paper.

- My family loves to celebrate birthdays.
- The birthday person gets to pick a special dessert.
- We all like to get together.
- The birthday person can ask for certain foods at lunch or dinner.
- We enjoy playing games on that day.

SEQUENCE (cont.)

☑ CHECK

Look back at what the word <u>sequence</u> means.

① Recall a holiday or other special day you celebrated together as a class. Talk about this day with your classmates.

② Write one thing you did during your celebration on an index card or as a note on an interactive whiteboard. 🖊

③ Work with classmates to <u>sequence</u> the events in the order they happened. Place your cards on a bulletin board or table, or drag and drop your notes on an interactive whiteboard to <u>sequence</u> what happened.

🔍 REVIEW

- When we <u>sequence</u>, we arrange things in an order that makes sense.
- We <u>sequence</u> events in a story in the order in which they happen.
- We can <u>sequence</u> or arrange things to show which object is next to another object.

💬 COLLABORATE

When we look back at what this word means, we see that it means to arrange things in an order that makes sense.

① What objects might you use to act out a family story? Your family story might be about a time you did something fun together or did something to celebrate a special day. How would you <u>sequence</u> those objects to tell the story?

_____

_____

_____

_____

_____

② On a separate piece of paper, draw pictures to show the objects. Use the pictures to <u>sequence</u> the events. Show and tell a partner how you <u>sequenced</u> the events to describe what happened.

③ Talk with your partner about the words we use to describe the <u>sequence</u> of people and things in a story. Think about where the people and things are compared to one another.

Name: _____

DISTINGUISH

 DEFINE

Question: What does it mean to <u>distinguish</u> between two things?

Answer: When we <u>distinguish</u> between two things, we tell the difference between them.

 STUDY

Sample Prompt: What is one way to <u>distinguish</u> between different kinds of trees?

Sample Answer: Some trees keep their leaves all year, and some trees lose their leaves.

Sample Prompt: How would you <u>distinguish</u> between plants that grow in the desert and plants that grow in a forest?

Sample Answer: Plants that grow in the desert live without very much water. They get a lot of sun. Plants that live in the forest often live in the shade. They get more water than plants in the desert.

✎ **PRACTICE**

① **Prompt:** How would you <u>distinguish</u> between a tree and a flower?

_____

_____

_____

② **Prompt:** <u>Distinguish</u> between a leafy tree and a bare tree. How would you describe each kind of tree?

_____

_____

_____

③ **Task:** <u>Distinguish</u> between the meanings of the words in **bold** below. Read each sentence and then describe what the word in **bold** means on the lines.

The tree had **thin** branches.

The tree had **scrawny** branches.

_____

_____

_____

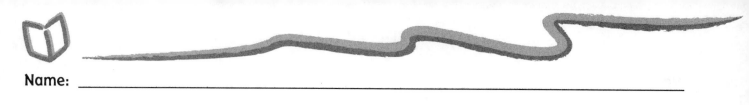

Name: _____

DISTINGUISH (cont.)

☑ CHECK

Look back at what the word <u>distinguish</u> means.

① Think about how you <u>distinguish</u> between different types of plants.

② Share your thoughts with a small group of classmates.

Use a separate piece of paper for the following group tasks:

③ Work together as a group to list things you notice about plants to <u>distinguish</u> between them.

④ How do we group plants? What do we call the different groups?

⑤ Refer to your notes to draw an example of one or more types of plants.

⑥ Discuss with your group your drawings and the groups of plants you <u>distinguished</u>.

🔍 REVIEW

- We can <u>distinguish</u> between two or more things by thinking about how they are different.
- When we <u>distinguish</u>, we notice the differences between people or things.
- We might separate things into groups by their differences to <u>distinguish</u> between them.

💬 COLLABORATE

When we look back at what this word means, we see that it means to notice the differences between two things.

① Trade page 90 (the first page of this lesson) with a classmate.

② Read your partner's answers for Practice Prompts #1 and #2. <u>Distinguish</u> the differences between your answers and your partner's answers.

③ How are the answers the same? How are they different? Why do you think there are differences?

_____

_____

_____

_____

④ Discuss your thoughts with your partner.

Name: _____

PERSUADE

 DEFINE

Question: What does it mean to persuade someone?
Answer: When we persuade someone, we make someone do or believe something. We do this by giving that person good reasons to do or believe what we say.

 STUDY

Sample Prompt: Persuade someone to watch a movie with you.
Sample Answer: You should watch a movie with me. It will be a fun way to spend time together. We can eat popcorn. After the movie is over, we can talk about why we like or don't like the movie.

Sample Prompt: How would you persuade someone to believe that *Frozen* is a good movie for kids?
Sample Answer: *Frozen* is an animated movie. It has many great songs in it. Kids can sing along to them. Most of the characters are friendly and funny.

✏ **PRACTICE**

① **Prompt:** What is your favorite movie? How would you persuade someone to believe this is a good movie?

_____

_____

② **Prompt:** What reasons could you give to persuade someone to watch your favorite movie?

_____

_____

_____

③ **Task:** Read the paragraph below. What reasons does the author give to persuade readers to watch *Beauty and the Beast*? Write your answers on the lines below the paragraph.

Beauty and the Beast has qualities that make it a good fairy tale. It has a magic castle. There is a bookworm and a beast. There are many surprises in the story. In the movie, things are not always the way they seem. We should look carefully to find out how something really is. As the saying goes, don't judge a book by its cover!

_____

_____

_____

Name: _____

PERSUADE (cont.)

☑ CHECK

Look back at what the word <u>persuade</u> means.

① Talk with classmates in a small group to decide on a movie you think other kids should see. Then work together to list reasons to <u>persuade</u> others to see this movie.

② Take turns presenting your reasons to another small group.

③ Which group's reasons would <u>persuade</u> more people to see a movie? Why? Discuss your answers in your groups.

🔍 REVIEW

- We <u>persuade</u> someone by giving good reasons to do or believe something.
- We <u>persuade</u> someone when we convince them to do or believe something.
- We can <u>persuade</u> someone to do something by asking them sincerely.

💬 COLLABORATE

When we look back at what this word means, we see that it means to give reasons for someone to believe or do something.

① Read a classmate's answers to Practice Prompts #1 and #2.

② Read the questions in the chart below. In the first blank shape, write the name of the movie your partner wrote about. In the second blank shape, list the reasons your partner gave for watching this movie. Color the circle to show your answer to each question. How many "yes" circles did you color? How well did your partner <u>persuade</u> you to think the movie he or she described would be a good movie to watch? Write your answers on a separate piece of paper.

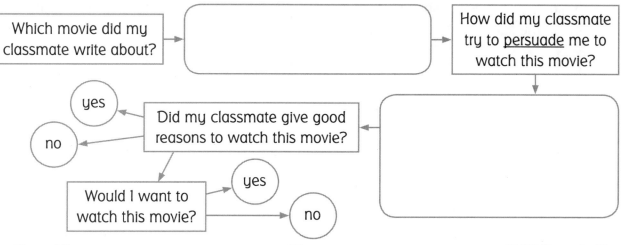

Name: _____

LABEL

 DEFINE

Question: What does it mean to <u>label</u> something?

Answer: When we <u>label</u> something, we give a word or phrase that describes it.

 STUDY

Sample Prompt: What word or phrase would you use to <u>label</u> a carrot?

Sample Answer: I would <u>label</u> a carrot as an orange vegetable. I could <u>label</u> it as a "natural food."

Sample Prompt: What are some words people use to <u>label</u> vegetables?

Sample Answer: People might <u>label</u> vegetables as "fresh," "healthy," "organic," or "grown close to home."

✏️ **PRACTICE**

① **Prompt:** Which words might you use to <u>label</u> green beans?

_____

_____

② **Prompt:** How would you <u>label</u> peas to give people more information about this vegetable?

_____

_____

③ **Task:** Read the paragraph below about broccoli. What words and phrases would you use to <u>label</u> this vegetable? Write your ideas in the box below the paragraph.

Broccoli is a green vegetable with stalks. There are small, green buds at the ends of the stalks. It grows best in fall or spring. Some people think it has a strong taste. Cauliflower and cabbage are in the same plant family as broccoli. People eat it raw or cooked.

LABEL *(cont.)*

☑ CHECK

Look back at what the word <u>label</u> means.

① With a small group, write a list of common vegetables.

② How would you <u>label</u> each vegetable to describe it? Talk with others in your group about the information you would give someone about each vegetable.

③ Work together to create an index card for each vegetable to <u>label</u> it as though it were in a grocery store. Make each card interesting and easy to read.

🔍 REVIEW

- When we <u>label</u> something, we use words to give information about it.
- When we <u>label</u> something, we put words or a name on it.
- We can <u>label</u> something by naming it or describing it in a certain way.

💬 COLLABORATE

When we look back at what this word means, we see that it means to use words to describe something.

① Draw pictures of your favorite vegetables.

② Trade papers with a partner.

③ <u>Label</u> the pictures your partner drew.

④ Why did you <u>label</u> each picture the way you did?

_____

_____

_____

Name: _____

RESEARCH

 ## DEFINE

Question: What does it mean to <u>research</u>?
Answer: When we <u>research</u>, we study to find out about a subject. We often read books about it or do experiments.

 ## STUDY

Sample Prompt: How could you <u>research</u> to learn about animal traits?
Sample Answer: I could read a book to find out what traits animals have.

Sample Prompt: <u>Research</u> one animal trait. What information did you learn?
Sample Answer: Some animals like to live in groups. This is a trait, or a way they live.

PRACTICE

① **Prompt:** What things can you use at your school to <u>research</u> a subject?

_____

_____

_____

② **Task:** On a separate piece of paper, draw a graphic organizer that will help you gather information when you <u>research</u> an animal.

③ **Prompt:** What kind of experiment could you do to <u>research</u> an animal?

_____

_____

_____

_____

④ **Prompt:** What do you think you will like about <u>researching</u> an animal?

_____

_____

_____

_____

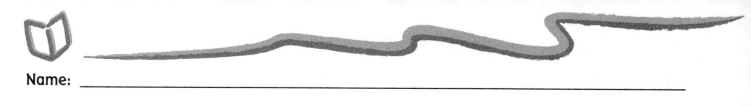

Name: _____

RESEARCH (cont.)

☑ CHECK

Look back at what the word <u>research</u> means.

① Work with a small group to <u>research</u> at least two special features of an animal. You might choose to <u>research</u> how that animal protects itself from danger, what it eats, or what things help the animal live in a certain place.

② Choose one way you will <u>research</u> the animal. Color one box below to show how you will <u>research</u>. Then <u>research</u> the animal.

I will read to learn new facts about the animal.	I will talk with someone else to learn about the animal.	I will look at pictures to learn about the animal.	I will find information about the animal's traits on an Internet site.	I will observe the animal by watching a video.

③ Use the graphic organizer you made for Practice Task #2 to take notes as you <u>research</u>.

④ Discuss your results as a group.

🔍 REVIEW

- We study to learn more about something when we <u>research</u>.
- When we <u>research</u>, we gather information about a subject.
- Sometimes people do experiments to <u>research</u> and find out about something.
- When we <u>research</u> a topic, we search books and other things to learn more about it.

💬 COLLABORATE

When we look back at what this word means, we see that it means to study something to learn more about it.

① Work with a classmate to create a list of words that describe what it means to <u>research</u> a subject.

_____

_____

_____

_____

② Create a poster to show others how to <u>research</u>. Include pictures or drawings to illustrate your poster.

Name: _____

RECOUNT

 ## DEFINE

Question: What does it mean to <u>recount</u> something?
Answer: When we <u>recount</u> something, we tell about it.

 ## STUDY

Sample Prompt: <u>Recount</u> something you have heard about castles.
Sample Answer: Castles were built a long time ago in other countries.

Sample Prompt: <u>Recount</u> an experience you have had with a castle.
Sample Answer: On a trip one time, I took a tour of what was left of a castle. There were a lot of stairs.

PRACTICE

① **Prompt:** <u>Recount</u> a story that happened in a castle. What happened in the story? <u>Recount</u> the events in order.

_____

_____

_____

_____

_____

_____

② **Task:** Read the story below. <u>Recount</u> the key details from the story on a separate piece of paper.

Once upon a time, a trader was traveling home. As he went through the woods, it began to get dark, and he lost his way. Suddenly, he saw a castle. He went in, hoping to find food and shelter. Each room was large and beautiful. But the castle was completely silent, and he saw no one. At last, he came to a cozy room with a fire in the fireplace and a meal set out next to a chair. He sat, ate, and warmed himself. Then he fell asleep.

③ **Prompt:** What lesson might readers learn from the story in Practice Task #2?

_____

_____

_____

RECOUNT *(cont.)*

☑ CHECK

Look back at what the word <u>recount</u> means.

① Think of a folktale or fairy tale you have read or heard. Talk with classmates to decide which story you will <u>recount</u>.

② Work together to <u>recount</u> the story. Take notes on an interactive whiteboard or chart paper as you try to remember as many details about the story as possible. Keep these questions in mind as you brainstorm with your group: 🖉
  • What events happen in the story?
  • What are the details in the story?
  • What is the main message or lesson in the story?

🔍 REVIEW

  • When we <u>recount</u> something, we tell about it in detail.
  • When we <u>recount</u> something, we tell about events in the order they happened.
  • When we <u>recount</u> something, we can also state the main idea, message, or lesson of the story.

💬 COLLABORATE

When we look back at what this word means, we see that it means to tell the events of a story in detail and in the order they happened.

① Think of a favorite fable or folktale you will <u>recount</u> for a classmate.

② Draw pictures to illustrate the ideas and characters' feelings in the story you will <u>recount</u>.

③ <u>Recount</u> the story to your partner, sharing your drawings as part of the story.

Name: _____

SUMMARIZE

 DEFINE

Question: What does it mean to summarize?
Answer: When we summarize, we give a short statement that tells the main ideas of something. We can summarize something that has been said or written.

 STUDY

Sample Prompt: Summarize what you know about insects.
Sample Answer: Insects are animals with three main body parts and six legs. They have one or two pairs of wings.

Sample Task: Summarize the sentences below.

Bees live all over the world. They help people by spreading pollen. This helps flowers bloom, and it also helps trees to have fruit. Bees also make honey. They are helpful insects.

Sample Answer: Bees are helpful to people because they make honey and help trees have fruit.

✎ **PRACTICE**

① **Prompt:** What information do we include when we summarize something?

_____

_____

② **Task:** Summarize the paragraph below in one or two sentences.

Ladybugs are not always red with black spots. Some are orange. Others have stripes instead of spots. Ladybugs have bright colors. These bright colors tell their enemies that ladybugs do not taste good. Farmers like ladybugs. These insects eat pests that hurt crops. The colorful ladybugs are helpful to people.

_____

_____

③ **Prompt:** Summarize what you know about ants.

_____

_____

_____

Name: _____

SUMMARIZE *(cont.)*

☑ CHECK

Look back at what the word <u>summarize</u> means.

① How would you <u>summarize</u> what you and your classmates know about butterflies? Take turns writing your ideas on chart paper or an interactive whiteboard. 🖊

② Follow along as your teacher reads the finished piece aloud.

③ <u>Summarize</u> the class writing in one or two sentences.

_____

_____

🔍 REVIEW

- We <u>summarize</u> when we give a short statement that tells the main ideas of something.
- We can <u>summarize</u> something that has been said or written.
- Sometimes people <u>summarize</u> ideas that have been said in a group.

💬 COLLABORATE

When we look back at what this word means, we see that it means to say or write the main idea of something briefly.

① <u>Summarize</u> in a few sentences an experience you have had with a spider.

_____

_____

_____

_____

② Trade papers with a partner.

③ <u>Summarize</u> your classmate's experience in one sentence.

_____

_____

④ Read your sentence back to your partner and ask him or her for comments.

Name: _____

REVISE

 DEFINE

Question: What does it mean to <u>revise</u> something?

Answer: When we <u>revise</u> something, we change or correct it. We might <u>revise</u> something to make it different.

 STUDY

Sample Task: <u>Revise</u> the sentence to make it correct.

> In winter, it is verry cold and Rainy.

Sample Answer: In winter, it is *very* cold and *rainy*.

Sample Task: Look at the sentences below. How did someone <u>revise</u> the second sentence to make it different from the first sentence?

1. In the fall, leaves fall to the ground.
2. In the fall, the wind blows bright red and yellow leaves off the trees.

Sample Answer: The second sentence has more action (the wind blows) and description (bright red and yellow...trees).

✎ **PRACTICE**

① **Prompt:** Why might we <u>revise</u> our writing? _____

_____

② **Task:** <u>Revise</u> these sentences below to make the writing stronger. Think about words that describe and other details you can add.

Summer is the best time of year because the sun shines a lot. People go on vacation and have fun.

_____

_____

_____

③ **Task:** On a separate piece of paper, <u>revise</u> the paragraph below to make each sentence correct. Check capitalization, spelling, and how each sentence ends. (*Hint:* There are four mistakes.) Add descriptive words and details to make the sentences interesting.

The weather changes ofen in the spring. You might see a rainbow. This happens when the sun Shines through raindrops Sometimes the rainbow has very brite colors.

REVISE (cont.)

☑ CHECK

Look back at what the word <u>revise</u> means.

① Read the first row of the chart. Write your ideas for each prompt in the second-row boxes.

② Ask two classmates what they think about the prompts. Write their ideas for each prompt in the third- and fourth-row boxes.

What I know about <u>revising</u> writing	Why we <u>revise</u> writing	How we <u>revise</u> writing

🔍 REVIEW

- We <u>revise</u> something when we change it or correct it.
- We can <u>revise</u> something by making it different.

💬 COLLABORATE

When we look back at what this word means, we see that it means to change or correct something.

① Read the paragraph below with a classmate.

Winter often brings storms when the wind blows and it rains. Some places get a lot of snow. In other places, the weather is not too cold. People also have different ideas about winter. Some people like it, but others cannot wait for summer!

② How would you <u>revise</u> the paragraph to make it a story? Write your ideas on a separate piece of paper.

ACADEMIC CONCEPTS GLOSSARY

On the activity pages, you may read some words that are new to you. This glossary has definitions for words you will see in the writing prompts and tasks. Always keep a copy of this glossary on hand as you complete each activity page.

academic (adj.) – having to do with study and learning

activity (n.) – something that you do

argument (n.) – a person's opinion about something

argumentative (adj.) – a type of writing that presents an argument

article (n.) – a piece of writing published in a newspaper or magazine

audience (n.) – the people who read a published piece of writing or who listen to a presentation

author (n.) – the writer of a story, book, article, play, or poem

author's voice (n.) – a writer's own way of using words that makes his or her writing different from others'

bibliography (n.) – a list of books an author used to research a topic

capitalization (n.) – the use of capital (uppercase) letters in writing or printing

caption (n.) – a short title or description printed with a drawing or photograph

category (n.) – a class or group of things that have something in common

cause (n.) – the reason that something happens

chapter (n.) – one of the parts into which a book is divided

character (n.) – one of the people (or an animal, creature, etc.) in a story, book, or play

characteristic (n.) – a quality or feature

chart (n.) – a drawing that shows information in the form of a table, graph, or picture

composition (n.) – a written work

comprehension (n.) – understanding

conclusion (n.) – the end of a story, article, or other piece of writing

connection (n.) – a link between people, objects, or ideas

context (n.) – the words around a specific word or phrase that help readers understand the meaning

conventions (n.) – the usual rules we follow to write English correctly

correct (adj.) – right

definition (n.) – an explanation of the meaning of a word or phrase

description (n.) – a picture created with words

detail (n.) – a small part of a whole item

diagram (n.) – a drawing or plan that explains something

dialogue (n.) – conversation, especially in a book or play

dictionary (n.) – a book that lists words in alphabetical order and explains what they mean

difference (n.) – the way in which things are not like each other

directions (n.) – instructions on how to do something; orders on what to do

discussion (n.) – a conversation about a topic to better understand it

effect (n.) – the result or consequence of something

effective (adj.) – working very well

essay (n.) – a piece of writing about a particular subject

event (n.) – something that happens, especially something interesting or important

evidence (n.) – information and facts that help prove something or make a person believe something is true

example (n.) – something typical of a larger group of things; a sample question given with the answer

ACADEMIC CONCEPTS GLOSSARY (cont.)

experience (n.) – something that happens to a person

expository (adj.) – a type of writing that explains something

fact (n.) – a piece of information that is true

feedback (n.) – comments and reactions to something

fiction (n.) – stories about characters and events that are not real

final (adj.) – last

folktale (n.) – a story that is told aloud and passed down from parents to children

graphic organizer (n.) – a visual display that explains how facts, terms, or ideas are connected
to each other

graphics (n.) – images such as drawings, maps, or graphs

idea (n.) – a thought, a plan, or an opinion

illustration (n.) – a picture in a book; an example

image (n.) – a picture you see or a picture you have in your mind

independently (adv.) – working with little or no help from other people

informational text (n.) – nonfiction writing that informs readers about a topic

instructions (n.) – directions on how to do something; orders on what to do

main idea (n.) – important information that tells something about the subject of a piece of writing

narrative (adj.) – a type of writing that tells a story

narrative (n.) – a story or an account of something that has happened

narrator (n.) – the person who tells a story

nonfiction (n.) – writing that is not fiction, especially information about real people, things,
places, and events

ACADEMIC CONCEPTS GLOSSARY (cont.)

opinion (n.) – the ideas and beliefs a person has about something

paragraph (n.) – a short passage that is about a single subject or idea

passage (n.) – a short section in a book or other piece of writing

peer (n.) – a person of the same age or standing as another

phrase (n.) – a group of words that have meaning but do not form a sentence

plot (n.) – the main story of a book, movie, or play

poem (n.) – a piece of writing arranged in short lines, often with a rhythm and some words that rhyme

point of view (n.) – an attitude, a viewpoint, or a way of looking at something

precise (adj.) – very correct or exact

previous (adj.) – what came before; former

problem (n.) – a difficult situation that needs to be figured out or overcome; a conflict

prompt (n.) – text that asks a person to do something or provide information

punctuation mark (n.) – a written mark, such as a comma, period, or question mark, used to make the meaning of writing clear

purpose (n.) – the reason why something is made or done

quality (n.) – a special characteristic of someone or something

reaction (n.) – an action in response to something

reason (n.) – something that makes something happen; why someone did a certain action; an explanation or excuse

relationship (n.) – the way in which things or people are connected

response (n.) – a reply or answer to something; a reaction

sample (n.) – a small amount of something that shows what the whole is like

ACADEMIC CONCEPTS GLOSSARY *(cont.)*

section (n.) – a part of something

sentence frame (n.) – a sentence with blank lines to give students a form to help them write

setting (n.) – the location where and time when a story takes place

similar (adj.) – alike or of the same type

solution (n.) – the answer or explanation to a problem

source (n.) – the place, person, or thing from which something comes

specific (adj.) – something exact or individually named

spelling (n.) – the way in which a word is correctly formed using letters

story (n.) – a spoken or written account of something that happened; it may be true or made up

summary (n.) – a short statement that gives the main ideas of something that has been said or written

table of contents (n.) – a list of titles of the parts of a book, listed in the order the parts appear in the book

thesaurus (n.) – a book that lists words in alphabetical order and gives related words that have the same and opposite meanings

title (n.) – the name of a book, movie, song, painting, or other work

trait (n.) – a quality or characteristic that makes one thing different from another

vocabulary (n.) – the words that a person uses and understands

LEXILE MEASURES

The Lexile® measures for the texts are listed in the table below. For reference, see the key that follows. It lists the Typical Reader Measures by grade level, as well as the Typical Text Measures by grade level.

Verb	Text	Page # in Book	Lexile® Measure
Review	Practice Task #2	16	450L
Take Notes	Practice Prompt #2	18	360L
Support	Collaborate	27	450L
Describe	Practice Task #1	30	470L
Identify	Practice Task #1	34	640L
State	Sample Prompt #2	40	370L
State	Practice Prompt #1	40	620L
Respond	Sample Prompt #2	50	490L
Examine	Sample Prompt #1	54	420L
Examine	Practice Task #2	54	380L
Brainstorm	Practice Task #2	56	640L
Demonstrate	Sample Task/Answer #1	62	550L
Demonstrate	Practice Task #1	62	470L
Predict	Practice Task #1	66	640L
Connect	Practice Task #2	68	520L
Conclude/Draw a Conclusion	Practice Task #1 – Fact Card #1	70	510L
Conclude/Draw a Conclusion	Practice Task #1 – Fact Card #2	70	470L
Conclude/Draw a Conclusion	Practice Task #2	70	620L
Select	Practice Task #1	72	600L
Inform	Practice Task #3	82	370L
Evaluate	Practice Task #3	84	470L
Persuade	Practice Task #3	92	520L
Label	Practice Task #3	94	540L
Recount	Practice Task #2	98	630L
Summarize	Practice Task #2	100	440L
Revise	Collaborate #1	103	440L

REFERENCE KEY: TYPICAL MEASURE RANGES FOR GRADE 2

Typical Reader Measure	Typical Text Measure (Text Demand Study, 2009)	Typical Text Measure (CCSS, 2012)
140L to 500L	450L to 570L	420L to 650L

MEETING STANDARDS

Each lesson meets one or more of the following Common Core State Standards © Copyright 2010. National Governors Association Center for Best Practices and Council of Chief State School Officers. All rights reserved. For more information about the Common Core State Standards, go to *http://www.corestandards.org/* or *http://www.teachercreated.com/standards/*.

Reading: Literature	Lesson
Key Ideas and Details	
ELA.RL.2.1: Ask and answer such questions as *who, what, where, when, why,* and *how* to demonstrate understanding of key details in a text.	Describe, Identify, Predict, Evaluate, Recount
ELA.RL.2.2: Recount stories, including fables and folktales from diverse cultures, and determine their central message, lesson, or moral.	Recount
ELA.RL.2.3: Describe how characters in a story respond to major events and challenges.	Identify
Craft and Structure	
ELA.RL.2.5: Describe the overall structure of a story, including describing how the beginning introduces the story and the ending concludes the action.	Sequence

Reading: Informational Text	Lesson
Key Ideas and Details	
ELA.RI.2.1: Ask and answer such questions as *who, what, where, when, why,* and *how* to demonstrate understanding of key details in a text.	Review, Take Notes, Support, Identify, State, Respond, Examine, Demonstrate, Inform, Label
ELA.RI.2.3: Describe the connection between a series of historical events, scientific ideas or concepts, or steps in technical procedures in a text.	Brainstorm, Connect
Craft and Structure	
ELA.RI.2.4: Determine the meaning of words and phrases in a text relevant to a *grade 2 topic or subject area.*	Define, Select
ELA.RI.2.6: Identify the main purpose of a text, including what the author wants to answer, explain, or describe.	Identify, Summarize
Integration of Knowledge and Ideas	
ELA.RI.2.8: Describe how reasons support specific points the author makes in a text.	Support, Connect, Persuade

MEETING STANDARDS (cont.)

Writing	Lesson
Text Types and Purposes	
ELA.W.2.1: Write opinion pieces in which they introduce the topic or book they are writing about, state an opinion, supply reasons that support the opinion, use linking words (e.g., *because, and, also*) to connect opinion and reasons, and provide a concluding statement or section.	Write, Practice, Explain, Support, Answer, State, Compare, Contrast, Respond, Examine, Brainstorm, Introduce, Participate, Connect, Select, Convince, Evaluate, Persuade
ELA.W.2.2: Write informative/explanatory texts in which they introduce a topic, use facts and definitions to develop points, and provide a concluding statement or section.	Report, Explain, Develop, Plan, Answer, State, Discuss, Give an Example, Examine, Introduce, Conclude/Draw a Conclusion, Inform
ELA.W.2.3: Write narratives in which they recount a well-elaborated event or short sequence of events, include details to describe actions, thoughts, and feelings, use temporal words to signal event order, and provide a sense of closure.	Tell, Produce, Describe, Identify, Order, Predict, List, Sequence
Production and Distribution of Writing	
ELA.W.2.5: With guidance and support from adults and peers, focus on a topic and strengthen writing as needed by revising and editing.	Plan, Compare, Order, Predict, Convince, Evaluate, Persuade, Revise
ELA.W.2.6: With guidance and support from adults, use a variety of digital tools to produce and publish writing, including in collaboration with peers.	Produce, State, Compare, Discuss, Select, Convince, Sequence, Recount, Summarize
Research to Build and Present Knowledge	
ELA.W.2.7: Participate in shared research and writing projects (e.g., read a number of books on a single topic to produce a report; record science observations).	List, Inform, Research, Recount
ELA.W.2.8: Recall information from experiences or gather information from provided sources to answer a question.	Tell, Respond, Recall, Sequence, Research

Speaking & Listening	Lesson
Comprehension and Collaboration	
ELA.SL.2.1: Participate in collaborative conversations with diverse partners about *grade 2 topics and texts* with peers and adults in small and larger groups.	*all*
ELA.SL.2.2: Recount or describe key ideas or details from a text read aloud or information presented orally or through other media.	Take Notes, Report, Discuss, Predict, Conclude/Draw a Conclusion, Select, Illustrate, Summarize
ELA.SL.2.3: Ask and answer questions about what a speaker says in order to clarify comprehension, gather additional information, or deepen understanding of a topic or issue.	Report, Explain, Develop, Answer, Discuss, Give an Example, Respond, Connect, Estimate, List

MEETING STANDARDS *(cont.)*

Speaking & Listening *(cont.)*	Lesson
Presentation of Knowledge and Ideas	
ELA.SL.2.4: Tell a story or recount an experience with appropriate facts and relevant, descriptive details, speaking audibly in coherent sentences.	Tell, Recall, Order, Connect, Illustrate, Sequence, Recount
ELA.SL.2.5: Create audio recordings of stories or poems; add drawings or other visual displays to stories or recounts of experiences when appropriate to clarify ideas, thoughts, and feelings.	Describe, Connect, Inform, Illustrate, Recount
ELA.SL.2.6: Produce complete sentences when appropriate to task and situation in order to provide requested detail or clarification.	Report, Explain, Develop, Produce, Answer, State, Discuss, Recall, Introduce, Demonstrate

Language	Lesson
Conventions of Standard English	
ELA.L.2.1: Demonstrate command of the conventions of standard English grammar and usage when writing or speaking.	*all*
ELA.L.2.2: Demonstrate command of the conventions of standard English capitalization, punctuation, and spelling when writing.	*all*
Knowledge of Language	
ELA.L.2.3: Use knowledge of language and its conventions when writing, speaking, reading, or listening.	*all*
Vocabulary Acquisition and Use	
ELA.L.2.4: Determine or clarify the meaning of unknown and multiple-meaning words and phrases based on grade 2 reading and content, choosing flexibly from an array of strategies.	*all*
ELA.L.2.5: Demonstrate understanding of word relationships and nuances in word meanings.	Identify, Determine, Compare, Match, Illustrate, Distinguish, Label
ELA.L.2.6: Use words and phrases acquired through conversations, reading and being read to, and responding to texts, including using adjectives and adverbs to describe (e.g., *When other kids are happy that makes me happy*).	Describe, Compare, Contrast, Brainstorm, Select, Match, List, Distinguish